Undertaking Discourse Analysis for Social Research

Kevin C. Dunn and Iver B. Neumann offer a concise, accessible introduction to discourse analysis in the social sciences. A vital resource for students and scholars alike, this book combines a theoretical and conceptual review with a "how-to" guide for using the method.

In the first part of the book, the authors discuss the development of discourse analysis as a research method and identify the main theoretical elements and epistemological assumptions that have led to its emergence as one of the primary qualitative methods of analysis in contemporary scholarship. Then, drawing from a wide-range of examples of social science scholarship, Dunn and Neumann provide an indispensable guide to the variety of ways discourse analysis has been used. They delve into what is gained by using this approach and demonstrate how one actually applies it. They cover such important issues as research prerequisites, how one conceives of a research question, what "counts" as evidence, how one "reads" the data, and some common obstacles and pitfalls. The result is a clear and accessible manual for successfully implementing discourse analysis in social research.

Kevin C. Dunn is Professor of Political Science at Hobart and William Smith Colleges.

Iver B. Neumann is the Montague Burton Professor of International Relations at the London School of Economics and Political Science and a Research Professor at the Norwegian Institute of International Affairs.

Undertaking Discourse Analysis for Social Research

Kevin C. Dunn and Iver B. Neumann

UNIVERSITY OF MICHIGAN PRESS | ANN ARBOR

Published in the United States of America by the
University of Michigan Press
Manufactured in the United States of America
⊗ Printed on acid-free paper

2019   2018   2017   2016   4   3   2   1

A CIP catalog record for this book is available from the British Library.

Library of Congress Cataloging-in-Publication Data

Names: Dunn, Kevin C., 1967– | Neumann, Iver B.
Title: Undertaking discourse analysis for social research / Kevin C. Dunn, Iver B. Neumann.
Description: Ann Arbor : University of Michigan Press, 2016. | Includes bibliographical
    references and index.
Identifiers: LCCN 2015033703| ISBN 9780472073115 (hardback) | ISBN 9780472053117
    (paperback) | ISBN 9780472121908 (ebook)
Subjects: LCSH: Social sciences—Research. | Discourse analysis.
Classification: LCC H62 .D7966   2016 | DDC 300.72—dc23
LC record available at http://lccn.loc.gov/2015033703

Contents

1 | Discourse Analysis in the Social Sciences   1
What Is a Discourse?   2
What Is Discourse Analysis?   4
How Is Discourse Analysis Different from Other Approaches?   9
Is Discourse Analysis the Right Approach for You?   11
Structure of the Book   14
Suggested Further Readings   15

2 | Variations in Theories and Approaches to Discourse Analysis   17
Defining Discourses   17
Theories of Discourses: From Structuralism to Postpositivism   21
    Structuralism   24
    The Frankfurt School and Poststructuralism   27
    Postpositivism   28
*Approaches to Discourse Analysis: Linguistic Studies and
Social Sciences*   30
    Discourse Analysis in Linguistic Studies   30
    Discourse Analysis in the Social Sciences   32
Suggested Further Readings   41

3 | Key Analytical Points   43
Language/Text   43
The Production of Knowledge   47
Discourses and Power   54
Representation and Practice   60
Discourse and Materiality   67
Subject Positions and Institutions   75
Suggested Further Readings   82

4 | Getting Started   83
Prerequisites   83
Conceiving a Research Question   86

Identifying and Selecting Sources   90
  Choosing Texts   91
  Delimiting Your Scope   94
  Variations in the Types of Texts   98
When Is Enough?   100
Suggested Further Readings   102

5 | Conducting Discourse Analysis   103
Different Strategies of Conducting Discourse Analysis   104
Identifying Discourses   105
Textual Mechanisms for Interpreting Discourses   109
  Presupposition and the Creation of Background Knowledges   110
  Predicate Analysis and the Creation of Subjects   111
  Subject Positioning   112
  Metaphorical Analysis   114
Inventorying Representations   116
Mapping Discourses   118
Layering Discourses   121
Suggested Further Readings   124

6 | Conclusion   125

Notes   131

Bibliography   135

Index   145

List of Boxes

Box 1   Michel Foucault, *Archaeology of Knowledge*   21
Box 2   Edward Said, *Orientalism*   48
Box 3   James Der Derian, *On Diplomacy*   52
Box 4   Achille Mbembe, "Provisional Notes on the Postcolony"   58
Box 5   Jens Bartelson, *A Genealogy of Sovereignty*   70
Box 6   Paul Willis, *Learning to Labour*   79
Box 7   Roxanne Doty, *Imperial Encounters*   89
Box 8   Lene Hansen, *Security as Practice: Discourse Analysis
         and the Bosnian War*   107
Box 9   Carol Cohn, "Sex and Death in the Rational World of
         Defense Intellectuals"   115

1 | Discourse Analysis in the Social Sciences

Discourse analysis is increasingly becoming a popular way in which scholars conduct social science research. Yet, there is often some understandable confusion given the wide array of assumptions, theoretical approaches, and research methods that get labeled "discourse analysis." This book seeks to be a concise, accessible introduction to discourse analysis in the social sciences. It is aimed at being a guide for graduate students, advanced undergraduates, and new scholars interested in expanding their research methods. In the chapters that follow, we will provide an overview of the development of discourse analysis in the social sciences, identifying the main theoretical elements and epistemological assumptions that have led to its emergence as one of the primary qualitative methods of analysis in contemporary scholarship. Ultimately, the book will help the reader understand the various ways in which one "does" discourse analysis.

In this introductory chapter, we begin by addressing a handful of key question. What is a discourse? What is discourse analysis? What are the variations in the ways one conducts and conceives of discourse analysis? How is discourse analysis different from other approaches of social science research? Is discourse analysis the right approach for you? As this is an introductory chapter, our answers to these questions will be somewhat sketchy, with the concepts, theories, and arguments we make here developed further in the following chapters. As with each chapter in the book, this introduction will conclude with a list of suggested further readings. Throughout the book, you will also encounter box inserts in which we briefly summarize exemplary discourse analyses to give you an awareness of the range of applications already employed by other scholars.

What Is a Discourse?

In very simple terms, a discourse entails the representational practices through which meanings are generated. Scholars who employ a focus on discourse often do so because they reject notions that knowledge is separate from the social realm and rather see knowledge as constitutive of reality. The material world does not present itself as self-evident to its inhabitants. Rather, societies construct and attach meanings and values to the material world around us. They do so through the construction of discourses. Analyzing discourses reveals how we come to take a certain phenomenon or an entire social reality for granted, and what kind of effects it has to naturalize that reality rather than another.

Most social science scholars working with discourses tend to go back to the foundational work of French theorist Michel Foucault, who understood discourses as constituting the objects of which they speak. Building on Foucault and theorists who have followed him, we understand discourses to be systems of meaning-production that fix meaning, however temporarily, and enable us to make sense of the world and to act within it.

We will go into a more detailed discussion of theories of discourses in the next chapter, but there are a few key points to flag at the outset. The first is to recognize the importance of **language**. Language can be regarded as a set of signs which are part of a system for generating subjects, objects, and worlds (Shapiro 1984: 222; Silverstein 2004). But language does not reveal essential truths. Rather, language is social, a series of collective codes and conventions through which things—objects, subjects, material realities, and so forth—are given meaning and endowed with particular identities (Hansen 2006: 18). Language does not explain the world as much as it produces it. The concept of discourse is an attempt at capturing how this happens. But, discourses cannot be equated exclusively with speech acts and textual products. Rather they are what make it possible for certain speech acts to appear as truth claims. As Foucault asserted, it is important that scholars analyze discourses by "no longer treating discourses as a group of signs (signifying elements referring to contents or representations) but as practices that systematically form the objects of which they speak" (1972: 49). Thus, to speak of a discourse may entail reference to specific groups of texts, but also to the social practices to which those texts are linked. Text should be understood broadly to include anything that carries the discourse, such as images, performances, and so forth.[1] It should be stressed at the outset that the text itself is not the object of study, rather discourse analysis uses text as a vehicle for understanding social, political, and cultural phenomena.

Second, discourses are both **structured** and **relational**: structured in the sense that they produce a field of intelligibility within the social realm, relational in the sense that this structure has no fixity, center, or permanence. Analytically, therefore, investigating the structure of a particular discourse helps scholars understand how particular "reality" becomes known and is acted upon. But to assume that a discourse is closed, static, and stable would be a mistake.

The third key point to remember is that, given their constructed nature, discourses are **open-ended** and **incomplete** or, to use a philosophical term, *emergent*. The partial fixity within a discourse enables one to "know" the world and act within the world based upon what one "knows," but a discourse is always shifting and never completely closed. A given discourse is always arbitrary and contingent. There is always space for contestation, which provides further analytical opportunities for researchers.

Fourth, the view that discourses are productive of "reality"—what can be known and acted upon—underscores the links between **knowledge** and **power**. Discourses function to naturalize meanings and identities by fixing particular representations, giving the impression of "truth." Language conveys meaning through the deployment of signs. As Jacques Derrida noted, "Every concept is involved in a chain within which it refers to the other, to other concepts, by means of a *systematic play of difference*" (Derrida 1981: 11; emphasis in original). The link between knowledge and power is revealed when there is an attempt to stop the signifying chain (at least temporarily) to give the appearance that a center exists and that meanings are fixed.

Finally, most scholars working with discourses understand them to be more than ideational, but to also have direct materiality because of the inextricable link to **practice**. For example, Jens Bartleson (1995: 71) notes that discourses are "systems of statements for the organization of practices." Because a discourse maintains a degree of regularity in social relations, it produces preconditions for action. It constrains how the stuff that the world consists of is ordered, and so how people categorize and think about the world. It constrains what is thought of at all, what is thought of as possible, and what is thought of as the "natural thing" to do in a given situation. But discourse cannot determine action completely. There will always be more than one possible outcome. Importantly, discourse analysis aims at specifying the bandwidth of possible outcomes.

Thus, we understand a discourse as a system producing a set of statements and practices that, by entering into institutions and appearing like normal, constructs the reality of its subjects and maintains a certain degree of regularity in a set of social relations. Or, more succinctly, *discourses are systems of meaning-production that fix meaning, however temporarily, and enable actors to make sense of the world and to act within it.*

What Is Discourse Analysis?

Discourse analysis has been described as "the close study of language in use" (Taylor 2001: 5). Discourse analysis entails an examination of how and why things appear the way they do, and how certain actions become possible. As we will discuss in future chapters, there are multiple research strategies scholars can and have taken in their work. In general, discourse analysts tend to interrogate the ways in which specific systems of meaning-production have been generated, circulated, internalized, and/or resisted. Often attention is focused on continuity, change, or rupture within specific discourses, either within a specific historical moment or comparatively (Mutlu and Salter 2013: 113–14). For example, we have each separately examined discourses of how a specific Self has constructed itself by constructing a certain Other: Iver explored the construction of Russia within Europe (1996), while Kevin examined the representations of the Congo in the Western imagination (2003). In doing so, we interrogated the persistence of certain linguistic signs and tropes, their transformations over time, as well as ruptures in the discourse that exposed marginalized voices and subjugated knowledges.

In order not to forget that these meanings are socially reproduced, discourse analysts often call them **representations**—stuff that is literally re-presented. Representations that are put forward time and again become a set of statements and practices through which certain language becomes institutionalized and "normalized" over time. They may be differently marked in terms of how influential they are. In the United States during the Cold War, "dove" and "hawk" representations of the Soviet Union were both institutionalized, but so was the (even less changing) representation of the Soviet Union put forward by the American Communist Party. When people who articulate the same representations organize, they make up a position in the discourse. Like representations, positions may be dominant or marginalized in various degrees.

Demonstrating institutionalized discourse can often simply be done by proving that metaphors regularly appear in the same texts. In Iver's study of European discourse on Russia, for example, he found a representation that stressed that Russian females had been raped by Mongol and Tatar males for centuries, and that this had fostered a particularly wild and barbarous people ("scratch the Russian, and the Tatar will emerge"). This representation began to form in France as that country was at war with Russia in the early 19th century, reached a peak in the interwar period (1919–39), and then lived a very submerged existence in Western European discourse. In the Baltic states, however, it was very strong indeed throughout the Soviet period and into the 1990s. The more such things may be specified empirically, the better the analysis. The ideal is to include as many representations and their variations as possible, and to specify where they are to be found in as high a degree as possible.

To illustrate these points about discourse analysis, let us take the concept of "juvenile delinquency." As a scholar, I might be interested in exploring how the concept has been defined and what policies have been engendered by different conceptualizations of juvenile delinquency. To do so, I may adopt discourse analysis. I would look at competing understandings of juvenile delinquency, how the language around it has been framed, by whom, and to what ends. I would also be interested in exploring how the meanings and practices associated with juvenile delinquency have changed over time and space. First, I would ask how, when, and where what came to be known as "juvenile delinquency" emerged as a concept in the first place. For example, I could explore how the concept has been defined and employed in late 20th century United States, or I could explore variations of the concept across different European countries. Then there is the question of the effects of defining and categorizing certain crimes in this rather than some other fashion. One such effect would be the emergence of special incarceratory institutions for people below 18 years of age. Regardless of how I chose to structure the research project, discourse analysis would be an effective social science research method to employ.

That said, if I were only interested in measuring the effectiveness of specific policies aimed at decreasing incidents of juvenile delinquency, then discourse analysis would not be an appropriate method. That is because such an approach assumes the stability of the concept, taking it as a given, natural fact. I would be making an ontological assumption that one can define and measure the related variables in an unproblematic way (ontology meaning what the world is taken to consist of). In such an approach, there is no need (or desire) to critically question the foundational elements of juvenile delinquency and any related concept. The process of meaning-making is taken as a natural fact. But if it is not, if one wishes to critically examine how juvenile delinquency as a concept is socially produced, then discourse analysis is a highly useful method.

Let us assume that I am interested in examining how the concept of juvenile delinquency gained political currency in postwar American culture. Adopting a discourse analysis approach might entail my examination of how language was employed at key moments in the development of the discourse. For instance, I might examine federal legislation that sought to address juvenile delinquency. It is within and around those events that the concept was defined and policies proscribed. To take but one example, in 1961, President John F. Kennedy signed the Juvenile Delinquency and Youth Offenses Control Act. At the time, he gave the following speech:

> I am happy to approve S. 279, Juvenile Delinquency and Youth Offenses Control Act of 1961. The future of our country depends

upon our younger people who will occupy positions of responsibility and leadership in the coming days. Yet for 11 years juvenile delinquency has been increasing. No city or State in our country has been immune. This is a matter of national concern and requires national action. With this legislation the Federal Government becomes an active partner with States and local communities to prevent and control the spread of delinquency. Though initiative and primary responsibility for coping with delinquency reside with families and local communities, the Federal Government can provide leadership, guidance and assistance (Kennedy 1961).

Within this very short speech and the attendant legislation, a discourse analyst might identify key elements of the discourse of juvenile delinquency. For example, concepts such as "juvenile," "youth," "delinquency," and "crime" are all presented, defined, and treated as natural facts. A problem (juvenile delinquency) is defined, its scale (national) delineated, and agents for solutions (families, local communities, and the federal government) identified. Rather than taking these important elements as natural facts, a discourse analyst would critically interrogate *how* they are produced and naturalized, and to what ends. The quote from Kennedy should not be treated simply as *the* discourse but part of the process in which discourses are manifested and at play. The reason why the terms in which the phenomenon is presented in this particular text seem so unproblematic at the time when they were uttered is that a lot of previous discursive work had already been done to make them so. Thus, an analyst should be sensitive to the fact that the object of study is a process, not a fixed structure. Examining American discourses of juvenile delinquency across the postwar era, for example, would indicate the ways in which discourses of race, class, and morality became intertwined in significant ways.

Briefly, the first research task is to identify discourses. This entails showing the affinities and differences between representations in order to demonstrate whether they belong to the same discourse. But repetition does not preclude variation or gradual re-presentation, so discourse analysts also seek to capture the inevitable cultural changes in representations of reality.

For example, in the late 1980s, Russia was obviously heading for challenging times, and Iver reckoned that this would entail wide-ranging changes in relations with Europe. His basic idea was that, regardless of period, Russia's relationship with Europe had not been straightforward, yet it seemed set to remain central to Russian foreign policy as well as to Russian self-understanding. Iver wanted to be able to say something general about prerequisites for Soviet/Russian foreign policy in a situation where so many things seemed to be in flux. Discourse analysis is eminently useful for such analysis, because it says something about why state Y was considered an enemy in state X, how war emerged as a political option, and how other options were shunted aside. In a particularly volatile historical moment, one way to get an analytical grounding is to look at the more or less deep-seated preconditions for how to represent "Europe" and "the West" in Russian discourse. The work done then was useful to understand the bandwidth of what could be said. As it happens, at the time of writing, twenty years later, it is still relevant to understand why the shrinking of possible ways of talking about "Europe" and "the West" in Russia takes the form it does, with Europe still being "decadent," "rotten," and so forth.

Broadly speaking, when conducting discourse analysis, the analyst tends to employ a three-step method. After identifying a discourse, one needs to delimit the discourse to a wide but manageable range of sources and timeframes. From these texts, the analyst then identifies the representations that comprise the discourse, taking into account censorship and other practices that shape the availability of text. Finally, to explore change, one uncovers layering within the discourse. The more actions that the analyst may account for by demonstrating their preconditions, and the more specifically this may be done, the better the discourse analysis. We will unpack these steps over chapters 4 and 5.

While discourses produce preconditions for action, they cannot determine action completely. Rather, they produce a parameter of possible actions. Thus, a discourse analysis approach moves away from an examination of empirical facts to an analysis of their conditions of possibility. As researchers ourselves, we have not employed discourse analysis to uncover grand "truths" about juvenile delinquency or Russian or Congolese identity. Rather, we have employed a social science approach to discourse analysis to investigate how meanings were produced and attached to various social subjects and objects, which in turn created certain possibilities for how to represent a phenomenon and precluded others.

Many scholars have come to believe that discourses are central to the production of social knowledge, as meanings are socially (re)produced through discourses. Yet, developing a coherent methodology of discourse analysis has been undermined by the various ways in which the term "discourse analysis" has been utilized by scholars to mean different things, both in terms of theory and practice. We will draw the differences out even further in chapter 3, but for now it is important to note that there are substantial differences between the ways in which discourse analysis is conceived and applied in linguistic studies as opposed to the social sciences. Of course, within the social sciences themselves, there is a fair degree of variation as well. For example, despite sharing a grounding in the insights provided by Michel Foucault (particularly in *The Archaeology of Knowledge*, 1970), there are differences between a social linguistics approach (see Fairclough 2003; Howarth and Stavrakakis 2000), which is primarily concerned with textual analysis, and a poststructuralist social science approach that maintains one can access social life through discourse (see Torfing 1999 and Bartelson 1995). The two approaches have different intellectual starting points, with the former driven by a belief that there is a discursive realm that is autonomously distinct from a nondiscursive realm. The latter rejects that there is an autonomous nondiscursive realm. The key word here is autonomous: it is not that nothing exist outside of discourse, but that in order to exist *for us*, phenomena have to be grasped *through* discourse. For poststructuralists, everything is filtered through discourse. While the two of us identify with the poststructuralist position, we stress that one need not adhere to poststructuralism in order to use discourse analysis. One can find utility in discourse analysis from a wide range of intellectual positions and analytical approaches. We will explore the differences between various approaches in chapter 3.

How Is Discourse Analysis Different from Other Approaches?

Discourse analysis tends to belong to the set of approaches generally labeled **qualitative**, as opposed to **quantitative**. Quantitative approaches in the social sciences tend to privilege the (usually numerical) measurement of an empirical reality. For example, studies focusing on voter behavior, the frequency of civil wars, or comparing the incarceration rates of black and white "juvenile delinquent" Americans can all be considered quantitative approaches. The assumptions often being made are that there is both an empirically recognizable reality and reliable scientific instruments of measurement that can be deployed to uncover universal and falsifiable conclusions about the social world.

Qualitative approaches are nonstatistical approaches that tend to be more textually based, often used to gain an understanding of underlying reasons and motivations for social phenomenon. To take the three examples noted above, a qualitative approach might use exit interviews to explore why certain voters made the choices they did, analyze speeches of political leaders to understand why a civil war erupted, or employ participant observation of troubled teens to better understand their issues and motivations.

Discourse analysis is a qualitative approach, but it has utility for researchers operating from both positivism and postpositivism. The degree of that utility and the ways in which discourse is conceived, however, vary significantly. **Positivism** holds that there is an empirically knowable world—both in the physical and social realm—that is governed by general laws. Positivists tend to maintain that, just as the material world operates according to absolute and universal laws, such as the law of gravity, so too does the social world (Jackson 2011). While positivists may employ both qualitative and quantitative approaches for inquiry, there is a tendency to privilege the latter because only quantitative data can be analyzed statistically, which is assumed to produce more rigorous claims to truth.

Postpositivists do not believe that human knowledge is produced by the scientific discovery of universal truths, but rather that it is socially constructed and contingent. They tend to assume that "reality" is unknowable outside human perception, and there is never only one authority on a given subject. As Friedrich Nietzsche noted in *Will to Power*, "There are no facts in themselves. It is always necessary to begin by introducing a meaning in order that there can be a fact" (1967 *KGW* viii I, 138; quoted in Barthes 1981: 16). A postpositivist position does not deny the existence of reality—that would be rather a stretch—but suggests that the "true" essence of the object is always unknowable to us. Therefore, we must interpret representations of it.

As we will explore in chapter 3, discourse analysis does not belong squarely in the exclusive domain of postpositivism. There are a number of positivist social scientists who employ discourse analysis in their work, most often under the distinctly misleading label "critical discourse analysis." We will explore the ontological distinctions between the various approaches to discourse analysis in that chapter, but for now it is worth recognizing the ways in which discourse analysis differs from other qualitative approaches within the social sciences.

Is Discourse Analysis the Right Approach for You?

When deciding whether or not discourse analysis is compatible with your research project, it is useful to begin with asking what form of questions are you interested in asking, because your answer will often have ontological and epistemological implications. One can make simple distinctions between what, why, and how questions. "What" questions often prompt historical narratives that assume a simple linearity of events. An example might be: what government policies and programs were put in place after JFK signed the 1961 juvenile delinquency legislation? "Why" questions tend to assume that a certain set of choices and answers preexist, and that a researcher only needs to come upon the right analytical combination to unlock the truth. For example, why did Republican legislators vote for or against the 1961 legislation? Both of these categories of questions are ill-suited for discourse analysis because essentially they either ignore the discursive realm or take it as an unproblematic given. Discourse analysis is best suited for answering "how" or "how-possible" questions. It focuses on social form and the general effects thereof rather than on specific outcomes. An example of such a question might be: how did juvenile delinquency become defined as a "national" "problem"?

Discourse analysis draws our attention to how options and the larger possibilities of action get established. Doing so allows for greater understanding of the processes and interactions within the social realm. Discourse analysis is suited for interrogating how meanings are produced and attached to various social subjects and objects, resulting in the production of certain interpretations that create a range of possibilities while precluding others. Again, a discourse constrains what is thought of at all, what is thought of as possible, and what is thought of as the "natural thing" to do in a given situation. Thus, a discourse analyst is interested in specifying the bandwidth of possible effects engendered by specific discourses. This works the other way, too; a discourse analyst may also start with a specific effect and demonstrate the preconditions for it happening, demonstrating concurrently that the effect might have been different if the discourse had been set up differently. As one might imagine, there are interesting issues and arguments regarding *causality* within discourse analysis approaches, which we will explore in chapter 3.

We should point out that significant limitations for doing discourse analysis arise from the scholar's ability to access the "data" of the discourse under examination. We will discuss strategies for identifying and acquiring sources of data in chapter 4, but it is useful to note at the outset some of the typical categorizations of data that have been employed by scholars. On one level, analysis can be conducted on "official" discourses—those texts and utterings by agents that society generally imbues with political power and significance. These can include speeches by political leaders and official state documents. For example, in her investigation of the United States' construction of insurgents in the Philippines at the end of the 19th century, Roxanne Doty (1996) examined archival records of official reports and publications. On another level, analysis can investigate the broader category of texts produced by socially recognized "experts," such as scholars. Edward Said's classic work *Orientalism* (1978) is driven by a discursive interrogation of how European scholars historically represented the "Orient" in general and the Middle East in particular. Depending on the subject matter, "expert" discourses can be produced by an array of agents. For example, Kevin has repeatedly examined how Western knowledge of Africa has been generated, which has led him to interrogate the colonial-era museum in Belgium and the popular travel writings of journalists such as Robert Kaplan (1994), both of which claim "expertise" in their own ways (Dunn 2003, 2004).

In addition to "official" and "expert" categories of discourse, one can also analyze what might generally be regarded as "popular" categories of discourse, which would include the study of popular cultural products like film, television, fiction, computer games, music, and photography. One of the assumptions scholars of discourses make is that discourses are the product of power by which hegemonic interpretations are seemingly naturalized and internalized, but also resisted and contested, within the social realm. If true, then one would expect the realm of popular culture to be rife with analytical potential, for popular culture fixes reality for a public that is broad by definition. Iver has engaged in an analysis of two popular culture forms—the Harry Potter cultural industry (Nexon and Neumann 2006) and the television show *Battlestar Galactica* (Kiersey and Neumann 2014)—while Kevin continues interrogations in the realm of popular music subcultures, namely punk (Dunn 2012 and forthcoming). Likewise, a discourse analyst interested in juvenile delinquency might engage with cinematic and literary representations of juvenile delinquency, such as *Rebel Without a Cause* (1955), *Rock'n'Roll High School* (1979), or *Kids* (1995). Note that the effects of popular culture may be global. A Norwegian criminologist, Liv Finstad (2000), spent a year riding with local police officers in Oslo, Norway. One of the things she noticed was that, upon being apprehended, a lot of "juvenile delinquents" tried to "take the fifth" (a reference to the Fifth Amendment of the US Constitution's protection against self-recrimination, aka the "right to remain silent"). Seeing that there is no such thing as taking the fifth in Norwegian law, this would appear to be a rather strange move, until one discovers that Norwegian TV channels broadcast a lot of American cop shows like *Miami Vice*, *L.A. Law*, and *N.Y.P.D. Blue*, where people seem to take the fifth in every other episode. For the Norwegian "juvenile delinquents" who tried to take the fifth, American popular culture discourse was a stronger constituent of reality than was Norwegian legal discourse. How you act when being arrested is no small matter, so the effects of this were important for the life chances of these people. Popular culture matters.

Our point is to both illustrate the varieties of ways in which one can engage in discourse analysis, regardless of the subject matter, and to draw attention to the importance of access and cultural competency. Discourse analysis might not be your best option if you do not have access to the categories of discursive data (official, expert, and/or popular) that you need, or if you lack the linguistic or cultural competency to adequately interpret them. For example, Iver's analysis of the bureaucratic mode of knowledge production in the Norwegian Ministry of Foreign Affairs was contingent on his ability to access internal notes, memos, and reports; his command of the Norwegian language; and his competency to "decode" the highly specialized language being employed within these texts (Neumann 2012). Kevin could not have conducted that particular research project.

Ultimately, discourse analysis is the right approach for you if you are interested in understanding how the seemingly unchanging and "natural" stuff of which our social worlds actually emerged as a creation of human history. Discourse analysis makes the social world more transparent by demonstrating how its elements interact. By demonstrating that things were not always the way they appear now, discourse analysis makes us aware that they are most probably changing even as we speak.

Structure of the Book

In the next chapter, we explore the various ways in which discourses have been conceptualized. First we offer a brief exploration of the ways discourse has been defined, before charting the development of theories of discourse from structuralism to poststructuralism to postpositivism. The chapter will then turn to a brief discussion of the differences and variations of discourse analysis in academia, specifically in the fields of linguistic studies and the social sciences. The chapter will then examine the various applications of discourse analysis within the social sciences, paying particular attention to the difference between a social linguistics approach and our social science approach. Exploring discourse as a postpositivistic method, we identify the ways in which discourses function as the part of the social world where meaning is constructed.

Chapter 3 is primarily concerned with discussing the analytical strategies used for studying discourses. Before we turn to a more developed discussion of the ways in which one can "do" discourse analysis in the following chapters, this chapter explores key elements: language/text; knowledge production; power; representations and practice; discourses and materiality; and subject positions and institutions.

In chapter 4, we cover the preliminary steps needed for successfully conducting discourse analysis. We present some observations about prerequisites before exploring how one conceives of a research question from the perspective of conducting discourse analysis. By drawing upon our own scholarship and other successful examples in the social science, we explore how one identifies and categorizes various sources of "data." We pay particular attention to concerns about how one chooses texts for analysis, how to delimit the scope of one's research, and questions related to different types of texts. We conclude with a few reflections on when the discourse analyst decides that she has enough research material.

Chapter 5 draws out how one conducts discourse analysis, driven by several empirical case studies (drawn from our own work as well as recent influential social science scholarship). After a discussion of the different strategies of conducting discourse analysis commonly encountered in the social sciences, the chapter offers a nuts-and-bolts discussion of employing a discursive analysis approach. We then offer an overview of the textual mechanisms for interpreting discourses, before turning to a discussion of locating discourses in a larger social and historical context. We conclude with a discussion of how one inventories representations and maps and layers discourses.

The final chapter reviews some of the key elements of the book and offers final advice for scholars embarking on discourse analysis.

SUGGESTED FURTHER READINGS

Andersen, Niels Akerstrom. 2003. *Discursive Analytical Strategies: Understanding Foucault, Koselleck, Laclau, Luhmann.* Bristol: Policy Press.
Fairclough, Norman. 2003. *Analysing Discourse.* London/New York: Routledge.

Foucault, Michel. 1970 [1969]. *Archaeology of Knowledge*. London: Tavistock.

Jackson, Patrick Thaddeus. 2011. *The Conduct of Inquiry in International Relations: Philosophy of Science and Its Implications for the Study of World Politics*. London/New York: Routledge.

Torfing, Jacob. 1999. *New Theories of Discourse: Laclau, Mouffe and Žižek*. Oxford: Blackwell.

2 | Variations in Theories and Approaches to Discourse Analysis

The purpose of this chapter is to unpack a number of the concepts related to discourse and discourse analysis that were introduced in the previous chapter. We begin with an overview of the various ways in which the concept "discourse" has been defined. We then briefly chart the evolution of theories of discourse from the development of structuralism to poststructuralism to postpositivism. The chapter then turns to a brief discussion of the differences and variations of discourse analysis in academia, specifically in the fields of linguistic studies and the social sciences. We then examine the various applications of discourse analysis within the social sciences, paying particular attention to the difference between a "critical discourse analysis" approach and a poststructuralist approach. Perhaps the primary distinction between the two is the former's assumption that there is a discursive realm that is autonomously distinct from a nondiscursive realm, a view that the latter rejects. Exploring discourse as a postpositivistic method, we identify the ways in which discourses function as the part of the social world where meaning is constructed. A focus on discourses is part of a broader "linguistic turn" in the social sciences, a scholarly development that recognizes that language does not reflect reality so much as creates reality. It is the recognition that language does not reveal a preexisting reality, but that language is what makes reality "real" in the sense of being understood and acted upon by humans.

Defining Discourses

In the introduction, we regarded a *discourse* as a system of meaning-production that fixes meaning, however temporarily, and enables actors to make sense of the world and to act within it. Admittedly, this conceptualization draws upon a number of previous writers, some like-minded but others quite divergent. To illustrate the range of conceptualizations of "discourse" we provide a few useful definitions:

- "practices that systemically form the objects of which they speak" (Foucault 1970: 49)
- "a system of dispersion between objects, types of statement, concepts, or thematic choices" that form "a regularity (an order, correlations, positions and functionings, transformations)" (Foucault 1970: 38)
- "a practice not just of representing the world, but of signifying the world, constituting and constructing the world in meaning" (Fairclough 1992: 64)
- "ways of being in the world; they are forms of life" (Gee 1996: viii)
- "sets of linguistic material that are coherent in organisation and content and enable people to construct meaning in social contexts" (Cohen, Manion and Morrison 2008: 389)
- "present as that which is absent; it becomes an empty signifier, as the signifier of this absence" (Laclau 1996: 44)
- "a system of statements in which each individual statement makes sense, produces interpretive possibilities by making it virtually impossible to think outside of it" (Doty 1993: 302)
- "systems of statements for the organization of practices" (Bartleson 1995: 71)
- "background capacities for persons to differentiate and identify things, giving them taken-for-granted qualities and attributes, and relating them to other objects" (Milliken 1999: 231)
- "a structure of meaning-in-use" (Weldes and Saco 1996: 373)
- "systems of meaning-production rather than simply statements or language, systems that 'fix' meaning, however temporarily, and enable us to make sense of the world" (Shepherd 2008: 10)

There is a perpetual struggle between different discourses to frame and define the categories and phenomena that constitute our world. To take but one example, until the end of the 19th century, sports were part of military discourse. This is hardly surprising since sports started as styliza-tion of battles (Elias and Dunning 1986). From the 19th century onwards, probably due to widespread democratization, sports increasingly entered cultural discourse. Over the last decades, it can be argued that sports have emerged as a discourse in their own right. Substantiation of this claim would involve investigating institutionalization of sports in ministries, coverage of sports in media, type of congregations where leading sports-men and women have appeared, and so forth. If there is an ongoing strug-gle about which discourse should frame which phenomena, it should come as no surprise that there also exists a struggle over the definition of the term discourse itself. Variations in the way the concept is conceived reflect ontological and epistemological differences, and also gesture to is-sues regarding its analytical deployment.

Ontology and epistemology are two concepts often used as building blocks when discourse analysts signal their disciplinary belonging and specify their approach. **Ontology** is the study of the nature of being—what the world consists of. A basic premise of discourse analysts' study of the social and political is that the world is in constant flux. It quite literally gives no meaning to claim what the world consists of, without specifying how it turned out to be like that, how it is maintained, and how it is challenged by alternatives. The discourse analyst is thus not primarily interested in the being but rather in how and why things appear the way they do.

Epistemology refers to how we obtain knowledge about the world. Such questions are essential to an analysis of discourse, while ontological questions remain in the background. Many other social science ap-proaches often isolate a part of the social world and define it as uncompli-cated (for example, through so-called independent variables), then use this frozen reality to say something about another part of the social world (for example, through so-called dependent variables). The advantage of such approaches is that they can say something substantial about a specific phenomenon, but in order to do so they objectify other aspects of the world. These moves are central to a methodology that is often privileged within these social science approaches. In order to distance themselves from such social science approaches, there have been calls from certain discourse analysts to reject terms such as "method" and "methodology," and talk about strategic problems instead.

Personally, we find this tactic to be highly problematic. In terms of the politics of academia, it is unwise to define "method" as a concept and a project to avoid, since the discourse on methods is saturated with the power to define what should pass as science and what should not. Voluntary excluding oneself from a discussion of methods means voluntary excluding oneself from a power resource, in addition to being exposed to attacks for not having a method. Instead of a revolutionary decapitation from the discourses on methods, working within it and with the intention to expand and transform it, seems to benefit the ideal of a pluralistic practice of science. Methods are often understood as representation from a certain point of view. Given that discourse analysis does not consider possibilities to find such a point of view other than in the social, from which an analyst may analyze something without being implicit, this description of methods is not only inappropriate in the case of discourse analysis but, due to its unrealizable nature, appears inappropriate in general (cf. Jackson 2011).

Returning to defining the concept itself, Fredrik Barth (1993: 173) defines discourse as a process reflecting a distribution of knowledge, authority, and social relationships, which propels those enrolled in it. Foucauldian Jens Bartelson (1995) defines discourse as "a system for the formation of statements." These definitions are more explicit than Foucault's own, which are supported by Nietzsche's view that only that which has no history can be defined. It can be said that Foucault intentionally plays a game of hide and seek with us. Only in the *Archaeology of Knowledge* does Foucault offer a few substantial signposts. In one place, he states that discourses are "practices that systematically form the objects of which they speak" (1970: 49). On the other hand, "Archeology describes discourses as practices specified in the element of the archive" (1970: 131), with "archive" being the whole range of preconditions that makes it possible to produce an utterance and have it accepted as a truth claim.[1] He also writes, rather mischievously:

> Instead of gradually reducing the rather fluctuating meaning of the word "discourse", I believe I have in fact added to its meanings; treating it sometimes as the general domain of all statements, sometimes as an individualizable group of statements, and sometimes as a regulated practice that accounts for a number of statements. (Foucault 1970: 80)

Definitions change with time and space. In this current situation of writing we could for example conclude that discourses are systems that produce a set of statements and practices that, by entering into institutions and appearing like normal, construct the reality of its subjects, and maintain a certain degree of regularity in a set of social relations. Or, to simplify, *discourses are systems of meaning-production that fix meaning, however temporarily, and enable actors to make sense of the world and to act within it.*

Theories of Discourse: From Structuralism to Postpositivism

In *The Archaeology of Knowledge* (1970), Foucault premises that a statement consists of what he calls an archive; that there is a set of enabling practices that may produce and maintain a given archive; and that the sum of this should be understood as discourse and analyzed by means of a method he calls archaeology. Foucault's initial privileging of discourse over practice, which he later reversed, lay him open to a charge from Dreyfus and Rabinow (1984: 84) that he was not able to account for change. The metaphor of archaeology suggests that layers simply lie there, to be uncovered by an analyst whose perspective must necessarily be extraneous to the reality studied. Foucault's answer to this problem was to move from discourse analysis to genealogy, which is one reason why we have sprinkled the text with references to the latter. There are other theoreticians that have contributed with interesting approaches, but *The Archaeology of Knowledge* is still a book that awards those who have time to read it carefully.

Box 1: Michel Foucault, *Archaeology of Knowledge*

The first methods lesson to be learned from Michel Foucault's book *Archaeology of Knowledge* (*L'Archeologie de savoir*, 1970) lies already in its gestation. Foucault enjoyed roaring success with his previous book, *The Order of Things* (*Les mots et les choses*, 1966), a book that analyzed the episteme or knowledge regime of the European 18th century and argued that its key principle was symmetry. Once Foucault was ensconced on sabbatical in Tunisia, he asked himself how he had actually come up with that analysis. The answer was *Archaeology of Knowledge*. We have here a reminder that good methods thinking may sometimes come only after the procedure has actually been carried out, as afterthought. Something to take heart from.

The key point of the book is the presentation of the concept of discourse. A discourse is a system for the formation of statements. Statements (or utterances, *enoncées*) purport to say something meaningful. That meaning is dependent on context. For example, "This water is holy" may mean nothing at all and so be a failed truth claim, or it may mean very different things in different contexts. Discourse is meant to be a concept for the context that fixes that content, for example, Hindu religious discourse, which would fix the water as water from the Ganges.

Discourse is itself an example of such a concept. Before Foucault, it simply meant speech, both in the sense of oral language communication and oratory delivered at an occasion. After Foucault, it means what makes such speech possible, in the sense of becoming meaningful.

Discourse was hatched in opposition to Claude Lévi-Strauss's concept of latent structure, where the idea is that one binary code underlies and founds the communication of society. What may be observed are manifest structures—for example, codes for what food to eat and how to cook it and for gendered division of labor. For followers of Lévi-Strauss, the job of the social scientist is to observe manifest structures in order to induce the underlying master code— the latent structure. By fastening on discourse instead of structure, Foucault in effect argued that there is no such thing as a latent structure. There are only different discourses. The upshot of such a way of seeing things is that nothing guarantees the wholeness of society. This was a critique of Lévi-Strauss's structuralism, but also a critique of Foucault's previous concept of episteme. This reflects the break between structuralism and poststructuralism. Note that Foucault only breaks with the determinism of structuralism and not with the general approach to social analysis. Poststructuralism is still a structuralism, so to speak.

In *Archaeology of Knowledge,* Foucault thought of discourses as a palimpsest or a canvas where different layers of painting exist on top of one another. Discourses may consequently be excavated, hence .the use of the archaeological metaphor. The old (Gr. *arche*) stuff to be excavated lay not in earth or on a canvas, but in what Foucault called the archive—in all different kinds of genres that is, the forms, mnemonics, and techniques which make saying, writing, and storing stuff possible (examples include ritual recital, pedagogics, festivals, public performance, and entertainment). The digging, or method of getting it excavated, was what came to be known as discourse analysis.

Foucault himself soon went from using an archaeological method to using a genealogical one, while Foucauldian discourse analysis went on to become a mainstay method in what the French call the human sciences.

One of the reasons why it has taken so long to develop methodological literature in this field is related to an intentional aversion to such a project, related to discourse analysts' desire to break down the distinction between methods and methodology, on the one hand, and theory, on the other. It is in this spirit, for example, that Jacob Torfing (1999: 292) warns of "the quest for a *methodology* able to utilize discourse theory in the concrete study of the construction of identity." Such an aversion appears to us as somewhat naïve. In our opinion, social scientists ought to relate to ontological and epistemological problems, and they should add to the type of knowledge produced by philosophers by engaging systematically with the world; that is, by doing empirical work. This added value comes primarily through development of methods and approaches capable of relating to the social, and through directly engaging with social practice. This applies even where it is difficult to sharply discern the distinction between theory and method, as is the case with discourse analysis. If all social scientists commit to meta-theory we risk leaving other important tasks to groups with even worse prerequisites to solve such problems than do social scientists.

We are in need of new literature on methods, exactly because we need a pluralistic array of means through which we can practice science. We should accept the uncertainty embedded in discussions on the distinction between reality understood as physical reality and reality understood as social representation, and devote scientific attention to the tensions involved in this distinction. Discourse analysis is one of several alternatives for those tasked with making this an empirical research enterprise, and thereby shedding light on those premises and conditions defining political practices. By recognizing these premises and conditions it is possible to gain a deeper understanding of specific political action.

An examination of the historical conditions that enabled discourse analysis would include the idea of a social science, of changing understanding of preconditions for human action, and about the development of the critical perspective. For our purposes here, we offer a brief discussion of three significant traditions informing discourse analysis: structuralism, the Frankfurt School, and postpositivism. Our goal is to provide the reader useful background knowledge for understanding the variations of discourse analysis discussed in chapter 3.

Structuralism

Discourse analysis is concerned with studying meaning, and it studies meaning where it occurs, that is, in language. Language is thus not seen as a straightforward system of concepts referring to things and phenomena directly, but rather as a social system that follows its own logic, and that this logic constitutes peoples' reality. This understanding attributes a relational logic to language. As the founder of modern linguistics, Ferdinand de Saussure (1986: 114) writes: "The content of a word is determined in the final analysis not by what it contains but by what exists outside of it." De Saussure's approach to language as a system of relations is a central precondition in discourse analysis. The so-called **linguistic turn** in the social sciences—the realization that language does not reflect reality so much as creates it—builds on de Saussure's idea that we can imagine relations forming or constituting language by considering relations as constituting all social things (see Silverstein 2004). De Saussure used the term discourse to refer to pieces of language longer than a simple sentence.

Within linguistics it is now more common to use discourse synonymously with verbal dialogue, for example, as conversation.[2]

The scientific tradition known as **structuralism** emerged in France, Russia, Czechoslovakia, and beyond, and was inspired by de Saussure as well as by the so-called formalism in literature. De Saussure differentiated between *langue* (language understood as a relational system) and *parole* (the spoken word, the specific act of language). Structuralism's prime thought was that a relational system in the form of a fixed grammar was hidden and latent in the social domain, and that this determined how manifested social interactions were structured.

De Saussure himself argued that it was *langue*—language as a relational system—that ought to be the object of linguistics. In addition to de Saussure and his followers' successfully institutionalized linguistic science of *langue,* Russian Mikhail Bakhtin began around the time of World War I to advocate for a science of *parole,* i.e., the "word" or the "discourse" defined as language in a vital and specific whole (Bakhtin [1963] 1993: 193). Bakhtin called this planned science *trans-linguistics.* Bakhtin's reason for establishing trans-linguistics is that we need a science about language that is able to say something about what he calls the dialogical relations between words, texts, and people. Bakhtin argued that linguistics was unable to do so because it considered a word independent of context other than the structure that connects it to the rest of the language, that is, independent of *social* context (Bakhtin [1963] 1993).

To Bakhtin, it is in the use of language that one may localize dialogical relations, and such relations exist between people, between people and text, and between texts *within* people. The dialogical is simply a way of being in the world. This is an ethical position. To prevent the sound of another person's voice is a metaphorical murder. Bakhtin was thus primarily concerned with what we now call **intersubjectivity** and **intertextuality** (he might also be considered the first to theorize the latter). That implied an assumption that texts necessarily enter into dialogue with other texts:

The historical life of classic works is in fact the uninterrupted process of their social and ideological re-accentuation. Thanks to the intentional potential embedded in them, such works have proved capable of uncovering in each era and against ever new dialogising backgrounds ever newer aspects of meaning; their semantic context literally continues to grow, to further create out of itself. (Bakhtin 1981: 421)

As such, Bakhtin preempted a general critique of structuralism that emerged in France toward the end of the 1960s, in which the principal point also was that one could not unproblematically assume that there existed a hidden enabling structure under the observable surface. That which could be studied, primarily language itself, was to be studied directly and in itself, just as Bakhtin had initiated nearly half a century earlier. It is here, in France at the end of the 1960s, and spearheaded by Michel Foucault, that discourse analysis understood as something different from and more than a pure linguistic text analysis emerged.

Structuralists, such as Claude Lévi-Strauss, thought of social analysis in three steps: (1) look at manifest (observable) structures and fixate them; (2) compare different manifest structures with a view to (3) identify latent structures, understood as the master structure that underlies a society and generates the different manifest structures. Foucault's *The Order of Things* and *Archeology of Knowledge* are key to the intellectual break between structuralism and poststructuralism. Poststructuralism broke with structuralism by denying the existence of something like latent structure. This meant that a new concept for what made observable structures possible, a concept that did not place the roots of the social outside of the social itself, was needed. The answer was discourse. The reader will now see why we insisted so strongly on there being nothing outside the discourse in the previous chapter; this supposition of what the world consists (and does not consist) of is the constitutive feature of poststructuralism.

There is a way in which poststructuralism's break with structuralism was a return to the scheme that Claude Lévi-Strauss had once rebelled against, namely that of Marcel Mauss and his teacher Émile Durkheim. Durkheim, the key figure in the institutionalization of the social sciences in France around the turn of the last century, wrote in his methods book from 1895 that the social was a special realm, that social phenomena should be analyzed in terms of other phenomena, that one should think about these phenomena as social facts, and that they should be treated analytically as things. Poststructuralism perpetuates all that. There is a clear affinity between Durkheim's concept of social fact and Foucault's concept of representation.

The Frankfurt School and Poststructuralism

Discourse analysis originates from an intense and direct rereading of structuralism—first by Bahktin's circle from 1910 onward, and then in Paris, and later in most places concerned with social theory from 1960 onward. Another scientific tradition that inspired discourse analysis in more indirect ways can be traced to discussions of the relationship between history and social sciences. The emergence of the Annales School was one of the most important developments in this context and influenced the development of discourse analysis (Dean 1994: 37–42). Named after the journal *Annales d'histoire économique et sociale*, the Annales School stressed an examination of social history that employed social scientific methods and emphasized social rather than political themes. When social sciences developed into more organized forms of inquiry from the middle of the 20th century, it adopted a certain position vis-à-vis history. Where history was to say something about specific sequences of events (be ideographic), social sciences were instead to discover universally applicable laws for human interaction (be nomothetic). Generalization was therefore a key preoccupation. This yielded an empty space between history and social science, a space for nonlaw and nonuniversal generalization that was soon filled by both sides, and often as a result of mutual inspiration.

The emergence of the so-called **Frankfurt School** was instrumental in the further development of discourse analysis in the social sciences. The Frankfurt School was a German interdisciplinary attempt at shaping critical theory—social theory not only intended at examining problems and suggest solutions within the frames of the established order but intended to burst the limits of invariance, that is to demonstrate that social variation is possible. Their analyses sought to show that the existing was not the only possible order, to uncover different ways of being in the world, to discover alternatives, and to contribute to social emancipation.

In 1983, the year before his death, Foucault declared, "If I had known about the Frankfurt School in time, I would have been saved a great deal of work. I would not have said a certain amount of nonsense and would not have taken so many false trials trying not to get lost, when the Frankfurt School had already cleared the way" (cited in Wiggershaus 1994: 4). Yet, the leading figure of the Frankfurt School from the 1960s until today, Jürgen Habermas, spent a lot of time trying to distance himself from and attacking Foucault, Jean-François Lyotard, and other discourse analysts. The debates emerging in the aftermath of Habermas's attack (see notably 1987) dealt to a larger extent with diagnosing the era (modern? late-modern? postmodern?) instead of questions of methods. They are however relevant in an introductory book about discourse analysis, because of the strong polarization between researchers from the two camps, which made interschool dialogue difficult. To be engaged in discourse analysis became what we would characterize as a completely unnecessary marker of belonging to a specific camp.

Postpositivism

While positivism maintains that there is an empirically knowable world governed by general laws, postpositivism asserts that human knowledge is socially constructed and contingent. Postpositivists tend to assume that "reality" is unknowable outside human perception, and there is never only one authority on a given subject. Again, Michel Foucault is useful here. Foucault proffered a thoroughly relational view of language. In his view, social relations are manifested in language and in those institutions constructed from certain ways of using linguistic categories. Here, the social scientists need not look "behind" language, for all is immediately given in the discourse:

> Nothing is fundamental. That is what is interesting in the analysis of society. That is why nothing irritates me as much as these inquiries—which are by definition metaphysical—on the foundations of power in the society and the self-institution of a society, etc. These are not fundamental phenomena. There are only reciprocal relations, and the perpetual gaps between intentions in relation to one another. (Foucault 1984: 247)

We can note a curious paradox here. One can define rather restrictively, and consider only the conscious recordable through sense-based data, and disregard other forms of consciousness or the prospective (there are other more refined ways of identifying a positivist that we will not deal with here; see Jackson 2011). It follows from this that one may argue that Foucault, who insists that social data are accessible in language, is a positivist. In a certain context he even went as far as calling himself a practitioner of joyful positivism (Foucault 1981). Three comments must however immediately be made here. First, we are talking about very different kinds of data. While social science traditionally regard data as made up of observations, discourse analysts relate to discourse, understood as merged text and social materiality. Second, in Foucault's "methods book" on archaeology, we find an approach that illustrates that the issue of structure and surface is not uncomplicated, even to him; some things are, if not fundamentally given, at least fundamental in the sense of being more stable than other things:

> This analysis of the "intellectual subconscious" of scientific disciplines is precisely Foucault's famous archaeological approach to the history of thought. Archaeology is an important alternative to standard history of ideas, with its emphasis on the theorizing of individual thinkers and concern with their influence on one another. Foucault suggests (and shows how the suggestion is fruitful) that the play of individuals' thought, in a given period and disciplinary context, takes place in a space with a structure defined by a system of rules more fundamental than the assertions of the individuals thinking in the space. Delineating the structures of this space (the goal of the archaeology of thought) often gives a more fundamental understanding of the history of thought than do standard histories centered on the individual subject (which Foucault disdainfully labels "doxology"). (Gutting 1994: 10; cf. Foucault 1970)

Third, there is significant coyness in Foucault's self-descriptions. A central tenet of his work is after all to demonstrate that the order of things easily could have been different. To him, the observable reality is contingent, and he does not privilege being over becoming, as positivists do. That said, Foucault and other postpositivists tackle the problem of reference by claiming that discourse refers to nothing outside of discourse itself. They bracket the nonsocial world or worlds—the pure materiality is simply not the referent object of discourse analysts—and instead devote interest to its representations. It is useful to recognize that this does not in any way imply a rejection of the material world as such; instead one claims that it is epistemologically and methodologically impossible to comprehend the nonsocial world directly and independently of representations. The positivist/postpositivist split has had direct implications on how discourse analysis is conceived and employed within the social sciences, which we explore below.

Approaches to Discourse Analysis: Linguistic Studies and Social Sciences

Discourse Analysis in Linguistic Studies

Unsurprisingly, there is a wide range of approaches to discourse analysis within the discipline of linguistics. Some are tied closely with the study of grammar. Others incorporate a focus on the ways in which ideas, issues, and themes are expressed in language more broadly. Within traditional linguistics, there has been a focus on the correlation of form with meaning, with discourse analysis exploring the ways in which meaning and understanding transcend simple sentence structure. In the late 20th century, **social linguistics** moved beyond the study of formal linguistic aspects to explore both the ways language is structured (grammar) and the social, cultural, and political aspects of language. For the past several decades, discourse analysis in the field of linguistic studies has been greatly shaped by the work of James Paul Gee (1999, 2005, 2011). For Gee, "discourse analysis is based on the details of speech (and gaze and gesture and action) that are arguably deemed *relevant* in the context where the speech was used *and* that are relevant to the arguments the analysis is attempting to make" (2011: xi).

Gee's *An Introduction to Discourse Analysis: Theory and Method* (1999, 2005) is considered a foundational text for the use of discourse analysis in social linguistics. Gee rejects structuralist assumptions that language un-problematically communicates information. For Gee, language serves two primary and closely related functions: "to support the performance of so-cial activities and social identities and to support human affiliation within cultures, social groups, and institutions" (2005: 1). In his work, Gee makes a distinction between "Discourse" ("big D") and "discourse" ("little d"). For Gee, "discourse" refers to language-in-use, while "Discourse" refers to when language interacts with other social practices (e.g., behavior, ges-tures, custom, eating, dressing, etc.) within a specific community.

For Gee, who is influenced by the works of Wittgenstein (1958), it is through discourse—"language-in-use"—that meanings are made, render-ing it both ubiquitous and political. Language has meaning only in and through social practices. Gee suggests that when one "pulls off" the per-formance of social identities and social activities—being an "X" doing "Y" (in one place Gee uses the examples of a gang member warning a member of another gang off his territory and a physicist convincing colleagues that a specific graph supports her ideas)—they do so through the use of language-in-use to convey meaning, but also by getting the "other stuff"—one's body, clothes, gestures, actions, symbols, values, attitudes, and so on—"right" as well. As Gee notes, "When 'little d' discourse (language-in-use) is melded integrally with non-language 'stuff' to enact specific identi-ties and activities, then I say that 'big D' Discourses are involved. . . . All life for all of us is just a patchwork of thoughts, words, objects, events, ac-tions, and interactions in Discourses" (Gee 2005: 7).

Thus, Gee conceptualizes "Discourse communities," and at any given moment people operate within different Discourse communities. For Gee, language-in-use (discourse) is a manifestation of the social construction of meaning. That is, Gee adopts a poststructuralist perspective that rejects the notion that language reveals any truths or centers. Meaning is con-structed through discourse and put into practice through Discourse. "Dis-courses, for me, crucially involve (a) situated identities; (b) ways of per-forming and recognizing characteristic identities and activities; (c) ways of coordinating and getting coordinated by other people, things, tools, technologies, symbol systems, places, and times; (d) characteristics ways of acting-interacting-feeling-emoting-valuing-gesturing-posturing-dressing-thinking-believing-knowing-speaking-listening (and, in some Discourses, reading-and-writing, as well)" (Gee 2005: 33). Significantly for Gee, the context in which discourse is employed/deployed is ultimately linked to power, especially given that societal power is unequally represented within different Discourse communities. In his works, Gee has developed an influential method (a "toolkit" in his terminology) for how one "does" discourse analysis, and we will return to a number of his "tools" in chapters 4 and 5.

Discourse Analysis in the Social Sciences

The basic assumption of much science is that senses are the only source of knowledge. It is claimed that humans know the world by seeing, hearing, and touching it. One specific way of knowing the world—the scientific—concerns finding regularities in these processes. We can imagine that the researcher collects a series of sense-based data. Based on these sense-based data, the researcher then makes a mental leap and postulates a theorem—a statement on regularities and a sketch for a truth. The theorem is often shaped as "if p, then q," or more often, "if p, then maybe q." The value p is often called an independent variable, while q is called a dependent variable. The thinking goes that by evoking supporting hypotheses and different methodological techniques it is possible to test the theorem, so that the researcher explores whether, or to which extent, there is consistency with new sense-based data through empirical research. The aim is often to universalize the theorem, so that it appears as universally "true." If new data show that it is not applicable in certain situations, it is falsified.

There exist scientific enterprises that do not assume that the only legitimate data are the positively given. From the institutionalization of social science at the end of the 20th century, and in particular in the last thirty years or so, much research has questioned the fundamental and assumed unquestionable premises of social science. These debates have primarily centered on questions of what can be considered given or real, and how it is possible to establish knowledge. In these debates about ontology (the being) and epistemology (knowledge production), a series of different and internally contradictory statements and positions have been proposed. Three are particularly relevant here.

First, it is not exclusively through the senses that humans try to understand or capture the world. If that were the case, one should expect certain regularity in the worldviews of different human societies. Traditional science's standard response to this criticism is that a scientific, sense-based way of relating to the world is superior to other ways, and therefore that it will suppress the other ways, as a scientific, rational worldview prevails. Yet, it cannot simply be assumed that all parts of humanity develop in this linear, parallel way, toward a defined goal. Moreover, the social scientist could, or should, try to study social reality from the inside, and from the vantage point of its own premises, instead of studying it through the social ideal offered by traditional science as a comparative basis.

Second, phenomenology has inspired many to point out that even if we reduce the entire spectre of human ways of grasping the world to perception and concentrate on that only, it is in fact impossible to directly grasp the world. Human perception is not immediate. From a chaotic amount of sense-based data, some are picked out. Perception, from the smallest practice and all the way to cosmology, is dependent on its organizing categories. As Thomas Kuhn observed, "something like a paradigm is prerequisite to perception itself" (Kuhn 1970: 113). Moreover, perception is not unmediated. Representations of the world enter between it and our grasping of it. In some cases there are blueprints for correct perceptions. In most cases, however, there are no such correct blueprints but rather negotiations over what is perceived. In order to create meaning, one mobilizes the already stored models, and sensations are presented to the perceiver as mediated by these models. At the same time we can say that the models themselves are re-represented, in the sense of instantiating social practice. The "models" are here socially reproduced facts, packages of phenomena that human cognition registers as wholes (Neumann and Neumann 2015), which we can echo in calling them **representations**. Representations are things and phenomena as they appear to us, that is, not the things themselves but things filtered through the fabric existing between the world and ourselves: language, categories, and so on. The discourse analyst makes it her task to show how representations are constituted and prevail, and the span of different representations that at any given time constitutes a discourse.

Finally, there are important considerations regarding the status of the perceiver. Traditionally, the researcher is represented as an observer looking in from the outside and passively downloading those aspects of reality as her theory indicates. The observer's social constitution is not questioned. This is one of the hallmarks of positivist social science. But as Michael Shapiro notes, it is no coincidence and neither a surprise "that a positivistic social science based on a philosophy of mind that regards consciousness, not as an active constituting force that constructs a system of entities, but as a passive recorder of sensations, would develop a view that the scientific observer may disregard the standpoint of subjects involved in conduct" (Shapiro 1981: 10). While postpositivists might agree that this lack of social positioning must be remedied, they disagree over the status attributed to a scientific observer and indeed to all subjects.

These ontological and epistemological differences have manifested themselves in the differing ways in which discourse analysis is regarded as a theory and method within the social sciences. Some social scientists have adopted a more linguistic-oriented approach in their work (see van Dijk 2001: 263). For our discussion, we focus on two variations that adopt a more social linguistics approach: the Critical Discourse Analysis (CDA) approach and approaches more broadly grouped under the category of poststructuralism.

Critical Discourse Analysis

Ultimately, the problem for social scientists interested in the study of discourses is to address the interaction between text and potential meaning. In general, social scientists have not necessary broken with linguistic insights but rather adjusted the linguists' lens. For example, Gunther Kress and Theo van Leeuwen (1996: 5) applied linguistic insights to nonlinguistic communication—in their case advertisement, children's toys, art, and other such phenomena. But they did so by also adopting many of traditional social science's epistemological and ontological positions (both in their positivist and structuralist manifestations). Such scholars, generally associated with a **Critical Discourse Analysis** approach, have helped bring discourse analysis into the mainstream of social science research. Critics of this approach sometimes claim that they are mistaken in trying to apply empirical/positivist beliefs of testability and scientific rigor to the study of discourses to make it more acceptable for mainstream social scientists. Certainly resistance to the "linguistic turn" in social sciences has been pronounced. In our own shared discipline of political science, discourse scholarship has been criticized as "bad" science because of its lack of testable theories or empirical analyses (e.g., Keohane 1988; Mearsheimer 1994/5). One notable scholar dismissed it as dangerous and seductive but ultimately "prolix and self-indulgent" (Walt 1991: 223).

We will unpack some of the arguments made by Critical Discourse Analysis by focusing on two of the ways in which they diverge from the poststructural social science approaches discussed in the next section. First, CDA assumes that there are two realms: the discursive and the extra-discursive. Second, they claim discourses can have a measurable degree of causality that often leads to claims of empirical rigor. Both positions are rejected by poststructuralists.

For many scholars, the "linguistic turn" in the social sciences did not entail a denial of a knowable reality outside of discourse. These researchers often position themselves as "realists" or "critical realists" to reflect their belief that an extra-discursive reality exists (Fairclough 2003; Rapley 2008). Pring (2000: 116) argues that the "acceptance of a reality independent of the researcher does not contradict the possibility of many interpretations of that reality." The position taken here is that there is an external reality—a material and social realm beyond language—that might be fixed and timeless, but because this realm is accessed through language—which is fluid, contingent, and temporary—the interrogation and analysis of language is an essential activity (see Coyle 1995: 243; Wetherell et al. 2001: 11).

The CDA approach assumes that there is distinction between the discursive and the nondiscursive (or extra-discursive) realms. As Fairclough argued, "these [discursive] practices are constrained by the fact that they inevitably take place within a constituted, material reality" (1992: 60). Thus, there is a "reality" that does not depend upon what is known about it (Sunderland 2004: 1). This approach understands human agency as existing within a dialectical relationship between discourses and social systems.

A significant proponent of CDA, Fairclough (1995: 2) offers a three-dimensional model that emphasizes the text ("the communicative event"), the discursive practices within which this text is embedded ("order of discourse"), and the social practices encompassing the order of discourse (the "social field"). Some have sought to connect Fairclough's three dimensions—textual, discursive, social—into separate exercises of *description, interpretation,* and *explanation* respectively (Titscher et al. 2000: 153). But in our reading of Fairclough, these three activities permeate each of Fairclough's dimensions, which he regards as intrinsically interlinked.

In general, the CDA approach sees a dialectical relationship between discourse and society but contends that discourses do not encompass all aspects of social life. For example, Chouliaraki and Fairclough (1999: 61) identify four "moments" of practices that they regard as "flanking" the discursive moment within social life: material activity (physical acts such as bombing, building, etc.), social relations and processes (class relations, the military-industrial complex, etc.), and mental phenomena (beliefs, values, etc.) (see also Banta 2013: 394). This framing enables scholars associated with the CDA approach to make empirical claims about discourses and causality. They tend to conceptualize discourses as "frames, . . . primarily instrumental devices that can foster common perceptions and understandings for specific purposes" (Howarth and Stavrakakis 2000: 3). These scholars believe it is possible to measure how effectively a discourse is utilized by people. Given the assumption of an extra-discursive realm discussed above, they assume that meaning is constant and identifiable through discourse. This structuralist ontological position leads CDA researchers to believe that not only do discourses have causal effects but that they can be analyzed through a focus on the structures of language and language-in-use (Shepherd 2008: 17).

CDA proponents and other critics of poststructuralist approaches often claim that poststructuralists are unnecessarily gripped with "epistemological trepidation" that leads them to antirealism, an acknowledgment of a "real world" but a rejection of any meaningful independence of it from our minds (Miller 2010 quoted in Banta 2013: 385). In contrast, CDA researchers maintain that what is real is "not exhausted by what is experienced or readily apprehensible" (Banta 2013: 389). As Bedau and Humphreys (2008: 1) claim, "There must first of all be structure to reality for it to have depth which we can uncover and make use of. Differentiation and materiality are dependent on a commitment to emergence in social phenomena, the latter meaning that there are objects that arise from and depend on some more basic phenomena yet are simultaneously autonomous from that base."

It is useful to examine some of the claims made by one of the best-known proponents of the CDA approach, Theo van Leeuwen. In his influential 2008 work *Discourse and Practice: New Tools for Critical Discourse Analysis*, van Leeuwen argues for the primacy of practice, contending that what holds modern societies together is no longer consensual meanings but common practice: "representation is ultimately based on practice, on 'what people do'" (van Leeuwen 2008: 4). As he argues further, "I will take the view that all texts, all representations of the world and what is going on in it, however abstract, should be interpreted as representations of social practices. . . . I will analyze all texts for the way they draw on, and transform, social practices" (van Leeuwen 2008: 5). In many ways, van Leeuwen is drawing upon Foucault's discussion of discourse: "They [discourses] not only represent what is going on, they also evaluate it, ascribe purpose to it, justify it, and so on, and in many texts these aspects of representation become far more important than the representation of the social practice itself" (van Leeuwen 2008: 6). But for van Leeuwen and like-minded CDA theorists, social practice also involves recontextualization: "Recontextualization not only makes the recontextualized social practices explicit to a greater or lesser degree, it also makes them pass through the filter of the practices in which they are inserted" (2008: 12). Recontextualization is an ongoing process and recontextualization leads to transformations. For van Leeuwen, there are a few kinds of transformations that can take place in the process of recontextualization: substitutions (resulting in new meanings being produced); deletions; rearrangements; and additions (2008: 17–18). Thus, discourse recontextualizes social practices by representing them in particular ways that ascribes new meanings to practices that alter their future iteration. **Causality** exists through the transformations produced within the recontextualization chain.

The claim of causality is sometimes tempered, sometimes replaced with "constant conjunctions" that operate as causal mechanisms (understood as any entity that produces a result) (Banta 2013: 390). Here the focus is on *tendencies* within which social entities combine to generate events (Kurki 2008). As Banta argues:

> For the scientific process of uncovering causal mechanisms, a distinction is made between the intransitive and the transitive. The former are the objects of scientific analysis, while the latter are the always-mediated discourses we use to describe them. Poststructuralists want to contend that all of society is transitive because the world is made real through discourse. [Critical realism/CDA] contends that discourses being analysed are intransitive *enough* to be studied as causal objects. (2013: 390)

Resisting charges of essentialism, CDA proponents claim that they recognize the mutability of essences but claim that they may also be stable enough to study, resulting in "always fallible but useful contingent generalizations" (Banta 2013: 390).

If you simply postulate that discourse has an anchor outside of itself, which Critical Discourse Analysts programmatically do, the methodological implication is a two-step process of analyzing the recontextualization chain. The first involves the analysis of the initial communicative event—such as an act, speech, or document—to expose how it tried to reshape or reproduce an order of discourse. Following this, recontextualizations of this event and the order of discourse are traced in real time to expose the degree in which some future social event(s) can be attributed to this initial process of discursive structuring. As Banta claims, "the analyst gains insights into the causal ability of a discourse and its 'discourse circle' to alter the order of discourse in one way or another, and connects this to theoretically salient features of extra-discursive practice" (Banta 2013: 394–95).

Poststructuralist Approaches to Discourse Analysis

We noted that Critical Discourse Analysts, such as Theo van Leeuwen, followed in the footsteps of structuralists by applying linguistic insights to nonlinguistic communication. Yet, from there it is just a small step to reach a central insight for poststructuralists: everything can be studied *as* text—as phenomena linked together by a code. This clearly does not mean that everything *is* text. But it implies that everything—gestures, monuments, films, dress, grave goods, and so on—can be read *as* text. Since language enters between humans and the world, there is nothing existing independent of text—there is nothing outside of text, nothing that can be comprehended regardless of text. This is a fundamental ontological position taken by poststructuralists that set them apart from the structuralist approach of Critical Discourse Analysis.

While both CDA and poststructuralist approaches claim Foucault as a touchstone, it is worth recognizing that Foucault's own thinking evolved. In his early work, Foucault spoke of three realms of relations, the first of which he considered to be comprised of "*real* or *primary* relations," which, "independently of all discourse or objects of discourse, may be described between institutions, techniques, social forms, etc" (1970: 44; emphasis in original). This implies that there exists a nondiscursive realm. Yet, in his later work he argues that there is nothing outside of the discursive realm (1977: 100). Poststructuralists adopt this latter position, maintaining that there is no distinction between a discursive and a nondiscursive realm. As Laclau and Mouffe write:

> Our analysis rejects the distinction between discursive and non-discursive practices. It affirms: a) that every object is constituted as an object of discourse, insofar as no object is given outside every discursive condition of emergence; and b) that any distinction between what are usually called the linguistic and behavioural aspects of a social practice, is either an incorrect distinction or ought to find its place within the social production of meaning, which is structured under the forms of discursive totalities. (2001: 107)

Discourse, in this sense, is treated as much more than language (that is, groups of signs signifying elements referring to contents or representations), but it also entails a focus on practices that, in the already quoted words of Foucault, "systemically form the objects of which they speak" (1970: 49). Some scholars, such as Torfing, refer to this poststructuralist approach as *discourse-theoretical analysis* (DTA) (1999: 12). The core concept here is that "reality" is produced and made understandable only through discourse. Unlike CDA scholars, poststructuralists do not believe there is anything outside of discourse. As Derrida provocatively formulated it, "*There is nothing outside of the text*" (1974: 158; emphasis in the original). As Foucault wrote, "Truth is a thing of this world. . . . Each society has its regime of truth . . . , the type of discourses which it accepts and makes function as true" (Foucault 1980: 131, 133).

It is worth stressing that poststructuralists are not rejecting a "real world" in which objects exist independent of our knowledge, rather it is only through discursive meaning-making that these objects become known and knowable to us. Laclau and Mouffe, for example, point out that the relationship between language and concepts are determined not by nature but by social processes, with signs only gaining their meaning within wider discourse structures, or "discursive totalities" (2001: 107). This point is echoed by Torfing, who argues that there is no "transcendental centre [i.e., referent] that structures the entire structure" (2005: 8). For social scientists, the result is that all the factors researchers examine—be they biological, psychological, institutional, and so forth—are discursively produced. Therefore, analysis is primarily about mapping discursive structures/institutions to show how they produce objects and subjects, how power relations are embedded and produced within discourses, and the ways in which discourses are related to practice and materiality. Methodologically, researchers shift away from attempts to uncover "truths" toward critically examining interpretations and the struggles for determining meanings (Yanow 1996: 19; cited in Shepherd 2008: 32).

In the spirit of transparency, we should state that we both identify with poststructuralist approaches to discourse analysis and with postpositivism more broadly. For us, there is no extra-discursive realm nor is it possible (or even desirable) to construct empirically falsifiable claims to scientific truth. As we proceed throughout the book, we will maintain this poststructuralist perspective. Note that the defining trait of poststructuralism is the ontological claim that the social world is in flux and cannot be grasped by maintaining a fixed point outside discourse. Logically, this point of view may invite a number of different political stances, from concluding that since a number of social worlds are conceivable, we may as well keep the one we have, to a revolutionary position where this world may as well be swapped for something very different. On the political plane, in practice, it is also worth noting that despite substantial ontological and epistemological differences, there are significant similarities between CDA and poststructuralist approaches to discourse analysis in the social sciences. For one, there are often similar ethical and political considerations driving the researchers. Both are interested in uncovering issues relating to power and domination, often with an eye toward exposing dominant ideologies and opening up alternative spaces. Van Dijk, for example, argues that the purpose of this "dissident research" is to "understand, expose, and resist social inequality" (2001: 352), a view we suspect resonates with many poststructuralists as well. The ways in which these different approaches conduct discourse analysis is also similar. In chapters 5 and 6, we will examine the ways in which social science researchers can "do" discourse analysis regardless of whether they identify with the CDA or poststructuralist approaches. This is not to suggest that methodological differences do not arise, and we will strive to flag those differences whenever appropriate. Our task is to help show some of the ways in which you can conduct discourse analysis in your research. We leave it up to you to sort out your own ontological and epistemological positions.

SUGGESTED FURTHER READINGS

de Saussure, Ferdinand. 1986 [1916]. *Course in General Linguistics*. La Salle, IL: Open Court.

Gee, James Paul. 1999. *An Introduction to Discourse Analysis Theory*. London/New York: Routledge.

Gee, James Paul. 2011. *How to Do Discourse Analysis*. London/New York: Routledge.

Laclau, Ernesto, and Chantal Mouffe. 2001 [1985]. *Hegemony and Socialist Strategy: Towards a Radical Democratic Politics*. London/New York: Verso.

Van Leeuwen, Theo. 2008. *Discourse and Practice: New Tools for Critical Discourse Analysis*. Oxford: Oxford University Press.

3 | Key Analytical Points

We maintain that all the factors that social science research examines—be they biological, psychological, institutional—are, first and foremost, discursive objects. Despite the important differences between approaches to discourse analysis (discussed in the previous chapter), there are key shared elements in how social scientists conceive and conduct discourse analysis. Where chapters 4 and particularly 5 address key methodological points concerning conducting discourse analysis, the purpose of this chapter is to give readers a sense of the significant analytical issues at stake. By no means exhaustive, the chapter seeks to underscore both the significance of these issues and their relevance for the methodological conversations that follow.

Language/Text

All approaches to discourse analysis begin with the assumption that discourses operate as systems of signification. Discourses are treated as a form of "data" to be analyzed, particularly as they produce social realities through the construction of meanings. Therefore, the key point of discourse analysis is to interrogate meaning as a part of the social world where meaning is constructed. It looks primarily at **language**, because other social practices (such as media, schooling, and family) produce meaning as a by-product, while language *primarily* intends to construct meaning (Shapiro 1988: xii). Through language, discourses produce background capacities for persons to differentiate and identify subjects/objects, to ascribe upon them attributes and values, and place them in relationship to other objects (Milliken 1999: 231).

For poststructuralists, language is significant, for it is only through language that the "things" that make up reality—objects, subjects, states, living beings, and material structures—are endowed with meaning and a particular identity. While positivist, empiricist science often assumes that language is a transparent medium for the dissemination and registration of information, poststructuralists regard language as a field of social and political practice. As such, there is no objective "truth" beyond linguistic representations (Shapiro 1981: 218; Hansen 2006: 18). For example, there is no "juvenile delinquency" until it is linguistically constructed. It is probably superfluous to do so at this point, but we should nonetheless like to repeat that the point is not that crime does not exist—it is a transhistorical (but not universal) fact that rules banning certain activities exist, that these rules are sometimes transgressed, and that some of these transgressions are singled out as grave enough to be in need of punishment. Beyond that, however, it is highly socially specific what a crime is, how perpetrators of those crimes are categorized, which crimes are singled out as being very grave and what is done by means of punishment.

These social practices can be read *as* **text**, that is, as systems of signs (which do not in any way reduce them to texts). When Jacques Derrida claimed that *"There is nothing outside of the text"* (1974: 158; emphasis in the original), he should be understood as cutting to the core characteristic of sociality: meaning is common, meaning cannot be reduced to something else, and ergo meaning must enter into all analyses of the social. The point is not that there is no "something" outside the text whatsoever but that this "something" must be traced according to how it appears as meaning socially. Concerning the relation between a text and its subject matter, poststructuralists maintain that there is no "additional text" or some sort of appendix that establishes a fixed connection or direct reference between the linguistic world and the world outside. For example, there is no *ur*-text that fixes the meaning of "juvenile delinquency." Again, it is important to note that the text is not the object of study. Rather, discourse analysis uses text as a vehicle for understanding social, political, and cultural phenomena.

Meaning is a precondition for action, and discourse analysis is committed to the study of these preconditions that ought to exist for action to take place. Meaning is therefore to be understood as traceable in language, not in each individual's mind. As Michael Shapiro has argued:

The language or system of signification is the system of the constitution of objects and events that emerge in speech as language is actualized. When persons engage in conduct, that conduct takes on a meaning or meanings as a result of the interpretations that are available in the language from which the interpreters select. When we therefore review the sets of constructs relating to conduct that exists in a language, we are viewing not only the horizons of possible speech but also the horizons of possible actions. The possibilities of action, then, exist in the language of a culture, and the actions that actually emerge are presented as a result of the controlling interpretations, those with general legitimacy. When we are speaking about those interpretations of conduct that produce and affirm actions and their concomitant subjects and objects that are institutionalized because the interpretation is oft repeated and accepted, we are speaking of "discursive practices." Discursive practices, according to Foucault, who treats them as his primary unit of analysis, delimit the range of objects that can be identified, define the perspectives that one can legitimately regard as knowledge, and constitute certain kinds of persons as agents of knowledge, thereby establishing norms for developing conceptualizations that are used to understand the phenomena which emerge as a result of the discursive delimitation. (1981: 130)

Thus, researchers conducting discourse analysis privilege an examination of language, not because it provides direct relations to universals truths but because it is within language that meaning-making and action-taking in the social realm are constructed and contested. As analysts, we are faced with the empirical question of exactly how language constructs meaning and acceptable/actionable knowledge.

Take the issue of "perception." President Kennedy perceived there to be a juvenile delinquency problem in America, but perceptions can never occur unmediated. The social world consists of a number of phenomena that appear in their specific form because the systems of constructing statements (the discourse) are of particular kinds. Social scientists adopting a positivist perspective often grapple with the idea that there is a set of right and wrong ways of comprehending the real and existing. This can be imagined as a perception and as misperception. The existing is then understood as correct, and the question is whether our references to the existing are right or wrong. This old philosophical problem is where we can locate the origins of discourse analysis. Phenomena (but not necessarily all stuff thought by someone) become social facts in and through language and institutionalization. Things are nothing by themselves; they are given meaning by entering into contexts with other things.

Language is thus the central system that is activated in the moment prior to perception. The shift in the social sciences beyond positivism is often described as a "linguistic turn"—toward the direction of a relational understanding of language—precisely to emphasize this. If language derives meaning from internal oppositions, as a relational understanding of language implies, then language is no longer subjected directly to human will. Each linguistic expression carries weight from previous relations with other linguistic expressions (understood as **intertextuality**). When JFK delivered his 1961 comments on juvenile delinquency, he was not inventing the concept out of whole cloth. Rather, his rhetorical moves depended upon preexisting representations and existing discourses. Roland Barthes argues:

> We know now that a text is not a line of words releasing a single "theological" meaning (the "message" of the Author-God) but a multidimensional space in which a variety of writings, none of them original, blend and clash. The text is a tissue of quotations drawn from the innumerable centres of culture [. . .] a text is made of multiple writings, drawn from many cultures and entering into mutual relations of dialogue. (1977: 143)

This insight has methodological implications for social scientists interested in employing discourse analysis, which we will explore across the following two chapters. For now, we want to stress the primacy of language, as well as its social constructedness and contingency, in the process of meaning-making, which will require that discursive studies empirically analyze language practices.

The Production of Knowledge

As social scientists, we privilege discourses because it is through discourse that the social world is produced. It is through discourses that subjects are both constructed and authorized to speak and to act. Discourses are comprised of signifying sequences that constitute more or less coherent frameworks for what can be said and done. Discourses provide a framework for understanding the world. Within discourses, representations construct "regimes of truth" or "knowledge." As Jennifer Miliken has observed, "discourses make intelligible some ways of being in, and acting towards, the world, and of operationalizing a particular 'regime of truth' while excluding other possible modes of identity and action" (1999: 229). Thus, discourses are intimately linked to the production of knowledge; they both enable and constrain. In general terms, discourses define subjects authorized to speak and act; define knowledgeable practices; produce objects; produce subjects as audiences; and produce so-called common sense.

There have been many examples of scholarly studies employing discourse analysis to reveal how certain structures of knowledge have been produced and entail political consequences. We have already mentioned *Orientalism* (1978), where Said explored how British and French societies constructed "truth claims" about the supposed innate and inferior qualities of nonwhite, non-Christian, "Oriental" people. Informed by Said and other like-minded scholars, numerous International Relations (IR) scholars have studied historical representations. Roxanne Doty's *Imperial Encounters* (1996) compares asymmetrical encounters between Great Britain and colonial Kenya with representations of the Philippines by the United States within its own imperial project. Cynthia Weber's *Simulating Sovereignty* (1995) traces how the meaning of sovereignty has shifted over time within discourses of intervention. As Weber notes, her discourse analysis approach is different from other theoretical approaches within IR because it examines "how foundations and boundaries are drawn—how states [or other entities] are written . . . with particular capacities and legitimacies at particular times and places" (1995: 29). Weber combines discourse analysis with Queer Theory and Lacanian psychoanalysis in her later book *Faking It* (1999), which playfully explores the representation of the Caribbean region in US foreign policy discourses. Unlike structural approaches in the social sciences, and IR specifically, these discursive approaches reject the idea that resources can be explained outside of their discursive context. The recognition of the productive power of discourses has important political and ethical implications because, by conducting discourse analysis, researchers denaturalize dominant forms of knowledge and open them up for critical interrogation, while also providing spaces for subjugated forms of knowledge.

Box 2: Edward Said, *Orientalism*

A very early and also very influential attempt at applying Foucauldian discourse analysis to the study of identity is Edward Said's 1978 book *Orientalism*. The basic idea is that "the East" is a constitutive outside for "the West," which means that the East is the Other from which the West has to delimit or limn its identity. As William Connolly formulated this basic point in 1991, identity demands difference to be and turns difference into Otherness in order to secure itself. Epistemologically, Said places the terrain on which this happens not in the psychic system, where many previous scholars had placed it, but in the social system. It is the social representations of the Other, and not the mental constructs thereof, that is of the essence. This has an immediate methodological effect in that textual and visual presentations become the place to look for the emergence of the Other.

Although Said, who was trained as a literary critic, investigates a number of genres, he singles out one specific genre, namely scientific writing, as particularly important. This is in keeping with Foucault's understanding of what he calls the power/knowledge nexus. Power/knowledge is a single entity. Knowledge, as a presentational system, is about producing social reality. This means that representation is productive; it has social effects. As a particularly cherished representational system, scientific knowledge is particularly productive.

In terms of method, Said's choice of texts to study is interesting in at least three ways. First, he chose texts about the region he, as someone with a Palestinian background, knew best, namely the Middle

East, and particularly the Arab world. Second, he chose texts written by the kind of people he knew best, and of which he himself was one, namely academics. Third, he chose texts written in the language of his own adopted country, namely English. All three choices have been criticized, but if we look at the choices in terms of discourse analysis, they make perfect sense. In terms of subject matter, texts to be studied must be about a phenomenon that one knows, for if one does not have the cultural competence, it is impossible to make sense of them. In terms of genre, this too demands specific knowledge on the part of the discourse analyst: if it is novels, it takes knowledge about the history of the novel, for each novel carries the memory of that history within itself and cannot be properly understood without it (one needs to know what plot is, what an authorial voice is, and so on). So it is with science. Our book is exactly an attempt to demonstrate and critique the history of a specific scientific subgenre, namely discourse analysis, so that each new discourse analysis may be better informed and, one may hope, self-reflective about itself. Finally, in terms of language, it makes sense to begin analysis by looking at the languages one knows best, and then proceed to widen the data looked at later. With respect to *Orientalism*, the book has been wildly successful in all three ways. Studies have emerged about "Orientalism" in different places (e.g., Ottoman and Turkish orientalist readings of Arabs), about other identities than have been represented as Other or Othered by English-language texts (e.g., Russia), and about representations of the Middle East and Arabs by Westerners in other languages, such as Italian and German.

In terms of effects, Said's *Orientalism* is what we may call self-referentially successful. It argues that scientific texts may be powerful by changing social reality, and the book has done exactly that. In scientific discourse, Orientalism now refers almost exclusively to the kind of subordinating Othering of "Easteners" by "Westerners" that the book critiques. There is a knock-on effect to political discourse, where the scientific debunking of Orientalism serves as a power resource for those who strive to counteract this kind of Western identity-building.

In addition to being successful in the sense of having spawned more work on the topic and in having contributed to the social and political solution to the phenomenon critiqued, the book has also been successful as one of the founding texts of a new genre of scientific endeavor, namely postcolonial studies.

A final point to make in terms of method is Said's explicit critique of Foucauldian discourse analysis for being too dismissive of specific texts. As Said puts it, "Foucault believes that in general the individual text or author counts for very little; empirically, in the case of Orientalism (and perhaps nowhere else) I find this not to be so" (Said 1978: 23). This points to the importance of what discourse analysts call monument critique, that is, the identification of certain texts as key or nodal to a discourse and the methodological problem of identifying such monuments of the discourse.

In order to critically interrogate the productive aspects of discourse, many discourse analysts engage what is often taken as "common sense" in the social world. For example, in Jutta Weldes's examination of "national security" within the context of the Cuban Missile Crisis, she employed an approach based on Stuart Hall that utilized concepts of *articulation* and *interpellation* to expose the ways that meanings were produced and "naturalized." **Articulation** refers to the construction of discursive objects and relationships out of a particular society's "cultural raw materials" and "linguistic resources" (Weldes 1999: 154). It is through the combining, recombining, and repeating that these "contingent and contextually specific representations of the world . . . come to seem as though they are inherently or necessarily connected and the meanings they produce come to seem natural, to be an accurate description of reality" (Weldes 1999: 154–55). **Interpellation**, then, refers to the processes through which these discourses create subject positions for individuals to identify with and to "speak from" (Weldes 1999: 163). One is interpellated or called into subject position: a subject position is specified and the subject fulfils it. Simone de Beauvoir's ([1949] 2011) famous analysis of how women *become* women might serve as an instructive example.[1] The result being that individuals come to accept these representations as natural and accurate, producing their social world.

Analytically, the discussion of discourse-as-productive raises important questions, particularly as structuralist and positivist approaches tend to impart causality to discourses because of their productive power (as discussed in the next section, "Discourses and Power"). Poststructuralists are wary of causal claims, but they do agree on the productive power of discourses. For some social science research agendas, there are also concerns about the operationalization of discursive categories—that is, the need to explore the connections between the production of policies and the implementation of those policies. Milliken (1999: 240), for example, suggests that many social science studies have displayed a failure to recognize the importance of operationalization within the study of discourse, while holding up Foucault's analysis of criminality (1977) as an exemplar for the study of policy implementation.

Generally speaking, researchers of discourse analysis examine the dominating/hegemonic discourses to illuminate both their structuring of meaning and the ways in which they are connected to implementing practices and actions. Thus, discourse analysts can examine the ways in which the production of knowledge appears to be stable and "natural." Methodologically speaking, one way to examine how constructed structures of knowledge become "naturalized" is through a **genealogical** approach, yet there is concern that such a method (over)emphasizes continuity. While it is important to note the production of "grids of intelligibility," it is equally important to note that these "grids" are always unstable. It takes work to "articulate" and "rearticulate" the produced knowledges and identities, to fix meanings and provide the appearance of stability. As such, it is useful for researchers to explore the ways in which discourses are changeable and historically contingent. Doing so opens up space for a researcher to explore subjugated knowledges. But, generally speaking, research on subjugated discourses has tended to be underdeveloped largely because it is often not articulated in English or other languages utilized by Western scholars.[2] Such research might also be highly localized (as Kevin's work on national parks in central Africa uncovered [2009]), which would require field research.

Finally, the purported productive power of discourse raises other important methodological questions, not the least of which is what counts as "cultural raw materials" and "linguistic resources" for different societies or within a society. If your research project engages exclusively with a highly specialized group of practitioners—such as Norwegian bureaucrats, Alaskan fishermen, or Colombian transvestite prostitutes—the linguistic resources will probably also be specialized, and your choice of discursive data should reflect that. But if your research project is less specialized, then other methodological choices will probably be needed. For example, in her article "Sex and Death in the Rational World of Defense Intellectuals" (1987), Carol Cohn was interested in examining the gendered dimensions of the professional discourses of defense analysts, which required a focus on a narrow slice of discursive production through internal reports and intra-office jargon—in similar ways to Iver's interrogation of the language utilized by Norwegian bureaucrats. But a more general examination of the production of "common sense" may best be served "by empirical study that examines 'mundane' cultural knowledge in specific contexts, and asks what resources it actually provides" (Milliken 1999: 239–40). One fruitful path may be to examine cultural products of "everyday life" (often understood as the popular culture realm) through which elements of "common sense" are embedded. We will explore these methodological issues further in the next chapter

---

Box 3: James Der Derian, *On Diplomacy*

James Der Derian's *On Diplomacy. A Genealogy of Western Estrangement* was published in 1987 by Blackwell. It was based on Der Derian's doctoral thesis at Oxford, which had been supervised by Hedley Bull. It is the first poststructural monograph within the discipline of International Relations (IR).

A genealogy is a history of the present. This means that the past is not treated in terms of how it leads to some future goal, say the Second Coming or the emergence of a classless society. Neither is the past treated in terms of reconstruction, as do Quentin Skinner and other so-called Cambridge Historians. The past is treated in terms of the present, that is, as a series of different sequences, some of which led us to where we are now.

The basic meaning of genealogy is the descent of an individual, via one's family tree. A key point is that people in that family tree who lived at the same time did not necessarily know of one another. They are only brought together and ordered as seen from the perspective of the person whose family tree it is. The only ones, if any, who have that particular descent would be full siblings. By the same token, any contemporary social phenomenon has a variety of preconditions for action.

These basic insights are summed up in three observations by the generator of genealogy as a scientific method, Friedrich Nietzsche, in *Genealogy of Morals* (*Zur Genealogie der Moral*, 1967 [1887]). Nietzsche argued that, like individuals, nothing has only one origin. He also postulated that there is always a dirty origin (*pudenda origo*)— some forefather or precondition that one would rather forget about. Also, only that which has no history can be defined—a definition freezes a phenomenon in a particular context, but given that historical contexts are forever changing, phenomena change with those contexts. It follows that a phenomenon, say "diplomacy," cannot be defined transhistorically beyond a minimum that considers the relations between polities. A genealogy is an attempt to pin it down. The method used is to read texts from the here and now, go back to when the phenomenon was certainly different, and then go forward again in order to identify the break. Once that is done, you start with the result and go further back, following the same procedure. The result is a series of periods, long- or short-lasting, divided by more or less abrupt breaks that together give us the "generations" of the phenomenon in question.

Der Derian does this for diplomacy, but he starts at the beginnings of writing and goes forward. The first period he calls mythic diplomacy—the entities mediated are God and his creation and the mediators are angels. The following periods are proto-diplomacy, diplomacy, anti-diplomacy, neo-diplomacy, and techno-diplomacy. The breaks between them are vague and non-final: "Occasionally, after a great conquest or defeat—be it military, diplomatic, or even technological—the historical flux seems to crystallize, sometimes long enough for us warily to speak of a paradigm" (Der Derian 1987: 70). For example, the spread of resident embassies among Italian city-states and then northward is part of the change from proto-diplomacy to diplomacy. The diplomacy paradigm is defined as a rei-fication of the idea of raison d'état.

If the goal is to attempt a full historical narrative or give historical background to a specific analysis, genealogy is an obvious choice for the discourse analyst.

Discourses and Power

Power is the *practice* of knowledge as a socially constructed system, within which various actors articulate and circulate their representations of "truth." For poststructuralists, language is constitutive for what is brought into being. As Hansen observes, "Language is social and political, an in-herently unstable system of signs that generate meaning through simulta-neous construction of identity and difference" (Hansen 2006: 17). Accept-ing that discourses are productive of knowledge acknowledges that there are inherent issues of power and ethics at play. Assuming an intrinsic rela-tionship between discourse and power, Milliken notes that "discourses are understood to work to define and to enable, and also to silence and to exclude, for example, by limiting and restricting authorities and experts to some groups, but not to others, endorsing a certain common sense, but making other modes of categorizing and judging meaningless, impracti-cable, inadequate or otherwise disqualified" (Milliken 1999: 229). Ulti-mately, a discourse constitutes the limits within which ideas and practices are considered, that is, delimiting what is the norm or normal, even natu-ral. Discourse's naturalizing power is largely unseen. Discussing Foucault's (1978) work on discourses, Trevor Barnes and James Duncan write, "The power of discourses derives not so much from the abstract ideas they rep-resent as from their material basis in the institutions and practices that make up the micro-political realm which Foucault sees as the source of much of the power in a society" (1992: 9).

Researchers adopting a poststructuralist position tend to understand power in ways articulated by Judith Butler: "power pervades the very conceptual apparatus that seeks to negotiate its terms, including the subject position of the critic; and further, that this implication of the terms of criticism in the field of power is . . . the very precondition of a politically engaged critique" (1993: 157). Thus, everything—every decision, representation, relationship, indeed every aspect of the social world—is a product of power relations and, thus, has a political aspect. Discourse analysis, especially from a poststructuralist position such as ours, gives analytical primacy to this conceptualization of power. As Shepherd argues, "It is this primacy of power that makes the approach so useful, whereby the 'polymorphous techniques of power' [Foucault 1978: 11] can be identified, problematized and challenged" (Shepherd 2008: 23).

We can begin by returning to the primacy of language for researchers. As language is relational, as argued by de Saussure (1986), one object is distinguished from another in the structured system. And as Derrida observed, systems of language—and discourses—are structured in terms of binary oppositions that establish a relationship of power through the privileging of one element in the binary (e.g., modern vs. traditional, good vs. evil). Since some representations become accepted as "true" and others do not, it is important to ask how certain structures of knowledge become dominant. Particular meanings and identities are widely accepted, or "fixed," not because of any inherent "truth" but because of the strength of that specific representation.

Building on Steven Lukes's "three-dimensional" approach presented in *Power: A Radical View* (1974), discourse analysis may be thought of as a "four-dimensional" approach to understanding power. Lukes begins with the claim that there is a fundamental resemblance between all concepts of power, namely that A affects B. He specifies that A influences B in a way that contradicts B's interests. This, according to Lukes, can be analyzed along three different "dimensions." A one-dimensional analysis looks at how A makes B do something he otherwise would not have done. The focus is on A's decisions on issues that concern B, and where B resists A in one way or another. One might develop such an analysis further by adding an organizational dimension. The two-dimensional analysis that then emerges will capture not only behavior but also the context of the behavior, that is, organizations (Lukes 1974: 16). It is significant that the organizational context within which A exercises power over B contributes to enabling and simplifying the exercise. The organization accommodates A's behavior and allows her to overrun B with less personal costs. But, Lukes goes on, what about those behaviors that do not meet resistance, because B simply does not know or does not wish that things could be different?

> Indeed, is it not the supreme exercise of power to get another or others to have the desires you want them to have—that is, to secure their compliance by controlling their thoughts and desires? [. . .] is it not the supreme and most insidious exercise of power to prevent people, to whatever degree, from having grievances by shaping their perceptions, cognitions and preferences in such a way that they accept their role in the existing order of things, either because they can see or imagine no alternative to it, or because they see it as natural and unchangeable, or because they value it as divinely ordained and beneficial? (1974: 23–24)

Lukes calls such analyses that incorporate such matters, in which even B's interests and preferences might be the result of a system that works counter to their interest, three-dimensional and radical (1974: 34).

Lukes's conceptions of power rest on the assumption that A influences B in a way that is contradictory to B's interests. Foucault's concept of power evades an acting "A" and instead focuses on how the order of things appears as *normal*, and therefore to some extent uncomplicated to *both* A and B. This normality generates a set of effects on patterns of behavior. Lukes's three-dimensional analysis emphasizes that B does not have full information of the structural bias that the behavioral context offers. An important point to Foucault and the four-dimensional discourse analysis is that neither does A have this complete information.

B's position is another significant difference between Lukes and Foucault, which also was a central tenet in Foucault's breaking with Marxism. Lukes talks about B's "interests" as something with a justification and relevance outside the discourse as such. The entire rationale of discourse analysis contradicts this way of thinking. Resistance is always something that originates in and is justified within the discourse, not something that exists outside it, such as the course of history, a religious order, a scientific sphere beyond time and space, and so on. The possibility of resistance against the hegemonic representations of discourse will always be present, whether by confirming alternative representations or even crafting new ones, or in the form of withholding confirmation, such as by silence or general impassivity. Critical scholarly approaches to discourse analysis can ask who constructs knowledge and truth claims, for what purposes, and against what resistance?

Another aspect of relevance in a discussion of power is the struggle over the applicable discourse in any given issue area. Terence Ball writes that political discourse is characterized by two key features:

First, political discourse borrows from and draws upon more specialised discourses; it is compounded, as it were, out of lesser languages. When the concepts and metaphors constituting the discourse of economics, for example—or of computer programming or law or religion or medicine or any other discipline—enter the field of political meanings they alter the shape and structure of that field by altering its speakers' terms of discourse. This process of transgressing, of leaking across discursive boundaries, is [. . .] a prime source of conceptual meaning. Second, political discourse characteristically consists of concepts whose meanings are not always agreed upon but are often heatedly contested by citizens-speakers. The possibility of communicative breakdown is an ever-present feature, if not indeed a defining characteristic, of political discourse. (1988: 12)

One can also investigate the workings of power in the production of discourses by exploring the struggle over who gets to speak authoritatively. External forces are constantly at play, seeking to select, plot, and interpret the events and meanings by which identities are represented. As Said noted, the dominant knowledge of "the Orient" was a creation of the

European imperial imagination. With its representations repeated over and over again in Western literature, government publications, and advertisements, Orientalism became *authoritative* knowledge.

Power is also exercised through the circulation process as competing discourses jockey for greater social acceptance and reproduction. There are often multiple and complex reasons for certain discourses gaining hegemony, and we believe it is important that a researcher be sensitive to these issues. Indeed, while discourses shape power, power also shapes discourse. Power, like discourses, is never totally centralized. A primary goal of this approach is to explore the relationship between discourse and power as they relate to representation. The significant points we would underscore here are: the multiplicity and contestedness of discourses; the complicated ways in which power works through the production and circulation processes; and the recognition that researchers are not neutral observers, but often are intimately related to the power hierarchies at play.

With regards to agency, discourse analysis assumes that people are guided to act in certain ways, and not others, by their discursively produced understanding of the world and their place in it (see Ringmar 1996). It rejects arguments that actors are motivated by inherent (universal) interests, rational means-ends preferences, or even internalized norms and values. It is admittedly limited in its ability to investigate issues of agency on an individual basis. But we tend to be skeptical that micro-level attempts at causal explanation offer better analyses because micro-level analyses usually ignore the effects of discourses as structures of meaning.

Box 4: Achille Mbembe, "Provisional Notes on the Postcolony"

Achille Mbembe, a Cameroonian philosopher and political scientist, published his seminal essay "Provisional Notes on the Postcolony" in the journal *Africa* in 1992. This essay, included in his 2001 collection *On the Postcolony*, was influential in the development of postcolonial scholarship. In this volume, Mbembe argues that Western academic and popular writings on Africa employ a range of tropes and clichés that reflect Western fantasies and fears. In these Western discourses, Africa becomes "the very figure of what is null, abolished, and, in its essence, in opposition to what is: the very expression of that nothing whose special feature is to be nothing at all." In many ways, Mbembe's assertion that "Africa" as a discursive product is constructed within the opposition of neither wholly itself nor wholly its absence is a rather conventional position within postcolonial scholarship. For our purposes here, what is notable about Mbembe's scholarship can be found in his article "Provisional Notes on the Postcolony," in which he argues that the "postcolony" is produced within the complexities of the discursive web that constructs everyday life and constitutes the postcolonial subject.

Mbembe employs a discourse analysis approach to read the "texts" of everyday life in Cameroon, what he calls the "postcolonial dramaturgy" (2001: 123), including media reports of a public execution, the display (and public shaving) of a goatee by a civil servant, state ceremonies, public dancing and singing for a state leader, and so on. Mbembe is particularly interested in ways in which discourse and practice are connected. As he writes, "I am concerned with the ways state power (1) *creates*, through administrative and bureaucratic practices, its own world of meanings—a master code that, while becoming the society's primary central code, ends by governing, perhaps paradoxically, the logics that underlie all other meanings within that society; (2) attempts to institutionalize this world of meanings as a 'socio-historical world' and to make that world real, turning it into a part of people's 'common sense' not only by instilling it in the minds of the *cibles*, or 'target population,' but also by integrating it into the period's consciousness" (2001: 103). He does this by looking at a range of symbols, signs, and narratives that are produced by state power, noting that the state attempts to both invest them with a surplus of meanings while simultaneously trying to fix their meaning.

Mbembe creatively analyzes the political discourses around the vulgar, obscene, and the grotesque, with an eye for how they are tied to the depictions and practices of power, as well as resistance and indiscipline. Mbembe's discourse analysis approach reveals a set of assumptions, orientations, expectations, and practices about the nature of authority and the exercise of domination that constitute life in the postcolony. But it also reveals ways in which discourses and state power can be creatively resisted from within the discursive structures themselves. For Mbembe, "the analyst must watch for the myriad ways ordinary people guide, deceive, and toy with power instead of confronting it directly" (2001: 128). As he notes, "What defines the postcolonized subject is the ability to engage in baroque practices fundamentally ambiguous, fluid, and modifiable even when there are clear, written, and precise rules" (2001: 129).

Representation and Practice[3]

Representations are inventions based on language, but they are not neutral or innocuous signifiers. Because they enable actors to "know" the object and to act upon what they "know," representations have very real political implications. Certain paths of action become possible within distinct discourses, while other paths become unthinkable. Discourses construct objects, subjects, and problems, but they also simultaneously articulate policies to address them (Shapiro 1988). Policies can be understood as discursively produced directions for action. As Hansen (2006: 21) writes: "Identities are thus articulates as the reasons why policies should be enacted, but they are also (re)produced through these very policy discourses: they are simultaneously (discursive) foundation and product." For an example, consider two photos circulated in the American media in the aftermath of Hurricane Katrina in New Orleans. The first showed a couple chest-high in water with bags full of groceries. The caption stated that this couple had "found" food in the wake of the hurricane. The second photo was of a similar scene, a woman chest-high in water with a bag full of groceries, but she was identified as a "looter." This disparity generated much attention because the "finders" were Caucasian while the "looter" was African-American. But even beyond the racial elements at work here, these representations had the effect of enabling and justifying certain actions. Police, for instance, would be expected to assist the couple and to arrest or even shoot the single woman. Thus, discursive practices create a truth-effect—"a doing, an activity and a normalized thing in society, one enjoining activity and conformity" (Brown 2005: 63)—that shapes the possibilities for action.

This example underscores the point that discourses, as structures of knowledge, establish preconditions and parameters for the possibility of action, rather than explaining why certain choices are made. For example, it helps a researcher understand the range of options imaginable to President John F. Kennedy during the Cuban Missile Crisis, but it does not explain why he made specific decisions (Weldes 1999). If one is interested in examining individual decision-making, one would either need to employ other methods or supplement discourse analysis with those other methods. But while there might be methodological compatibility, one should be sensitive to the possible existence of an epistemological divide on the issue of causality. As we discussed earlier, scholars operating within an approach such as Critical Discourse Analysis might be comfortable imparting causality, but poststructuralists tend to adopt "a logic of interpretation that acknowledges the improbability of cataloguing, calculating, and specifying 'real causes'" (Campbell 1993: 7–8).

Like any fully fledged approach to social research, discourse analysis has to own up to the challenge of studying how humans make their own history, but not under conditions they themselves have chosen. The analysis of discourse understood as the study of the preconditions for action has to be complemented by analysis of practice understood as the study of action itself. Some scholars may maintain that such a turn to practice is unnecessary, especially given that, since the world cannot be grasped outside of language, there is nothing outside of discourse, and for this reason the analysis of language is all that we need in order to account for what is going on in the world. Such a response would, however, rather miss the point, for what is at stake is not the question of whether there exists something outside of language. Practices are discursive, both in the sense that some practices involve speech acts and in the sense that practice cannot be thought "outside of" discourse. Our concern is how best to analyze social life *given that* that life can only play itself out in language. Just because the social is inextricably immersed in and suffused by language, it does not follow that we have to limit our methods of studying it to those that access the social through language. This is a *non sequiteur*, and a politically pacifying one at that.

Discourse analysts have consistently grappled with the dilemma of how to reconcile meaning and materiality, discourse and practice. Foucault saw practices as being part of the discourse, hence he wrote about discursive practices, with discourse being the privileged concept. The tendency to privilege discourse over practice has since been intensified by discourse analysts such as Laclau and Mouffe. Practice theorists reverse this conceptual hierarchy by taking the material understood as practice as their point of departure.

A central challenge for social analysis, then, must be how to preserve the insights that have been produced by the linguistic turn while also adding the insights promised by practice theory, to combine the study of meaning and the study of the material. One way of doing this is to place culture at the center of the analysis and to conceptualize it as a dynamic interplay between discourse and practice. Discourse may then be understood as a system for the formation of statements, while practices are "socially recognized forms of activity, done on the basis of what members learn from others, and capable of being done well or badly, correctly or incorrectly" (Barnes 2001: 19). The latter aspect is important because it pinpoints that practice is something more than habit. If discourse refers to preconditions for action and practice to patterns of action, then discourse and practice together should add up to a concept of culture. As Theodore Schatzki (2001: 44) puts it, discourse "is being, while practice is the becoming from which discourses result and to which they eventually succumb. Conversely, discourses are the precarious fixities that precipitate from human practice and from which further practice arises. The latter formulation is preferable [. . .] because practice has form (being) only in so far as it issues from extant discourse."

Note that such a reconceptualization is dynamic both in the sense that it introduces an understanding of change rather than stasis as the "normal" state of affairs, in the sense that it focuses on empirical change, and that it places discourse and practice in two different time tracks by letting them emerge in different ways. Ann Swidler (2001: 85) argues that practices "re-

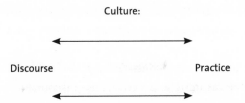

Fig. 1. Culture understood as a dynamic interplay between discourse and practice

main stable not only because habit engrains standard ways of doing things, but the need to engage one another forces people to return to common structures. Indeed, antagonistic interchanges may reproduce common structures more precisely than friendly alliances do" (Swidler 2001: 85). What has been done so far may be summed up in figure 1 above.

It may be useful to revisit the work of one of Foucault's contemporaries, the social anthropologist Michel de Certeau. Contrary to Foucault, de Certeau's aim was to establish a theory of action, with a focus on how things are used. His basic unit of analysis was not the utterance but the action. In order to understand everyday actions, de Certeau focused on the tacit knowledge that goes into performing them and perhaps altering them, all the tricks and improvisations that come into play and which are traditionally read out of social analyses (1984: 20). Given the existence of discourse, and given that practices are embedded in one another, it must be possible to establish what kind of repertoire of actions exists for a particular type of subject in a particular type of context. De Certeau (1984: 82) also reintroduced an old Greek term, *metis*, which refers to ways of comportment, ways of behaving in the world, ways of acting and thinking where the point is to "obtain the maximum number of effects from the minimum force." *Metis* refers to the perfectly timed, seemingly natural and seemingly effortless quality of an action. The anthropologist James C. Scott, who has taken de Certeau's project further in a number of different ways, defines *metis* as "a wide array of practical skills and acquired intelligence in responding to a constantly changing natural and human environment" (1998: 313).

De Certeau forged his concept of *metis* as a resource with which to critique his by now more famous contemporaries Foucault and, particularly, Bourdieu (1977; 1991). Bourdieu focuses on how practices emerge by starting with a structure, which yields a *habitus* (an incorporated mode of being in the world), which yields a set of strategies. When these strategies are employed, they meet a set of conjunctures, and the result of this meeting is a set of renewed structures. De Certeau highlights two problems in this way of setting up the analysis. First, Bourdieu presupposes that practices are unequivocally bound in space, that geography and administrative practices go hand in hand. This is a presupposition that de Certeau (1984: 55–56) finds unwarranted in an age of what we would now call globalization. Second, de Certeau charges Bourdieu with reifying practices. Bourdieu still works in the spirit of the nation-state and holds culture to be a unitary phenomenon, so that a population and its territory appear as a seamless thing. To de Certeau, culture cannot be unitary, and so the practices that are part of it cannot be incorporated in each subject in the same way. Instead of looking at the interplay of practices and geographically bounded structures and practices as does Bourdieu, we should look at the dynamic interplay of discourse and practices. De Certeau (1984: 125) himself examines the role of what he calls *stories*: "stories 'go in a procession' ahead of social practices in order to open a field for them." Stories, chunks of discourse, make possible a practice. Things are ordered, subject positions created, and these and other phenomena named so that a practice that is new in the relevant context may take shape. This practice is nested in other practices, both in the sense that it emanates from a set of similar practices existing elsewhere and in that it has to fit in with other practices that already play themselves out in the new field into which they are being inserted. Let us call the kind of power that goes with extending the discourse of which you are a part by establishing new practices or maintaining already established ones conceptual power.

As the new practice is being adopted, two things happen. First, since this new practice has to fit in with other already established practices, they are altered: there are omissions, additions, and creations. These alterations are large enough for the new practice to fit in to the new domain, but not so large that the new practice may no longer serve as a conduit between that domain and the domain from which it was extended in the first place (if that happens, then the practice is no longer socially tied to the discourse from which it emanated). Second, as the new practice is institutionalized in the sense of becoming regular and a more seamless part of the social, it is also naturalized. As a naturalized social force, it emanates stories of what things should be like. The practice speaks: "this is how we have always done things around here." For example, this is what Margaret Somers (1994: 614) seems to have in mind when she writes that "people are guided to act in certain ways, and not others, on the basis of the projections, expectations, and memories derived from a multiplicity but ultimately limited repertoire of available social, public, and cultural narratives." The social fact that things are ordered in a particular way and not another may be conceptualized as a story that tells specific people what to do in specific contexts. A phenomenon that makes people do what they would not otherwise have done is a phenomenon of power. In this case, it is a power that makes it possible to govern people indirectly and from afar, by impinging on their schemes of action by instituting a new practice. Let us follow the late Foucault (2000) and call this form of power **governmentality**. As long as people act in accordance with established practices, they confirm a given discourse (as seen from the governor's point of view, they are well governed). The possibility also exists, however, that people will *not* act in accordance with a given practice, in which case discourse will come under strain (see Mbembe 1992). We can now elaborate on the model given in figure 1 as follows in figure 2.

To sum up, practices are integrative, inasmuch as they nudge human beings into relationships of amity and enmity. They "remain stable not only because habit engrains standard ways of doing things, but the need to engage one another forces people to return to common structures. Indeed, antagonistic interchanges may reproduce common structures more precisely than friendly alliances do" (Swidler 2001: 85). They are improvising, inasmuch as they play themselves out in concrete situations for which humans may only be partially prepared. They are reflective, inasmuch as they have to relate to the actions of other actors (to what extent they are conscious is, however, a contested matter). They are quotidian, in the sense

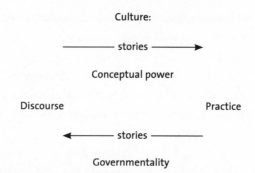

Fig. 2. Culture understood as a circuit of practice, discourse, and stories, charged with power

that they play themselves out every day, often in seemingly trivial ways, and are part of everybody's lives. They are performative—they *are* their use—and they are stylized.[4]

The possibility of accounting for a range of contemporary social and political phenomena thus requires treating discourses and practices together, as preconditions for action and patterned action respectively. It is within the interaction between discourse and practice that researchers can make methodological interventions. As Shepherd argues, "If discursive practices both manifest and construct discourse through (re)presentation and (re)production, then practices of (re)presentation and (re)production are the sites at which it is possible to locate power in a given discursive terrain. Thus [discourse analysis] is concerned with representation as a source for the (re)production of knowledge" (2008: 24). Discursive practices "maintain, construct and constitute, legitimize, resist and suspend meaning, and it is these practices that theorists can analyze" (2008: 21). With regard to methodological strategies, Shepherd offers three possibilities: double reading, analysis of theoretical schemata/nodal points, and analysis of prediction/subject-positioning (2008: 21). By contrast, Miliken (1999: 242–43) has noted four main methods for interrogating the connections between discourse and practice:

(1) *Deconstructive method*, through which the contingent nature of a discourse is revealed through close textual analyses that ex-

poses and troubles the poles of opposition employed within a
text to privilege and producing "truths";

(2) *Juxtapositional method*, which juxtaposes the "truth" produced
within a particular discourse to events and issues that this
"truth" fails to deal with, often by comparing the dominant representations with contemporaneous accounts utilizing alternative interpretations and "truths";

(3) *Subjugated knowledges*, which works off of the juxtapositional
method to explore in greater alternative accounts that are mark-
edly different from the hegemonic discourse;

(4) *Genealogical method*, which offers a historical examination that
exposes the contingency of contemporary discursive practices
by treating that "as a series of discursive formations that are dis-
continuous, breaking with one another in terms of discursive
objects, relations, and their operationalization" (Milliken 1999:
243).

These methods will be unpacked in greater detail in chapter 5.

Discourse and Materiality

As the previous section on discourse and practice illustrated, the "linguistic turn" within the social sciences reorients the study of social interaction
to where it actually takes place, namely in language, but also raises issues
about materiality. Discourse should not simply be reduced to the realm of
ideas; discourse incorporates material as well as ideational factors. Language as such has a materiality.

For our purpose, the problem is *not* to establish the autonomous nature of language as a social system, or as an epiphenomenon that unques-
tionably imitates the material. As Hansen argues, "the point is not to disregard material facts but to study how these are produced and prioritized"
(2006: 22). As she continues, "The strategy of discourse analysis is thus to
'incorporate' material and ideational factors rather than to privilege one
over the other. . . . The analytical intent is not to measure the relative im-

portance of ideas and materiality but to understand them as constructed through a discourse which gives materiality meaning by drawing upon a particular set of identity constructions" (2006: 23).

The main purpose of discourse analysis is to propose a method that is able to analyze the linguistic and material holistically. This is done by understanding discourse as both a linguistic and a material phenomenon. Yet, the difference between the linguistic and the material does not thereby disappear. The problem is to develop the discourse concept to find ways of studying them both. The intention is to study how preconditions exist for verbal and physical action, how a given statement activates or initiates a series of social practices, and how the statement in turn confirms or disproves these practices. Foucault states that these preconditions for action are determined by "the archive," so that "the set of rules which at a given period and for a definite society defined: 1) the limits and forms of expressibility; 2) the limits of forms of conservation; 3) the limits and forms of memory; and 4) the limits and forms of reactivation" (1981: 59–60).

As we understand it, the materiality of text is linked to the archive. It concerns such matters as whether a storage medium such as script is used or not, what type of script is used (e.g., alphabetic), what kind of language is used and which sociolects and dialects of this language are used, and who has the linguistic competence to benefit from the archive. More specifically, one may look at the extent to which the concept of books is related to publishing by publishing houses, the number of published copies, and so forth. In Norway, for example, the number of books published by publishing houses rose from about 2,500 to more than 4,000 over the last twenty years. Given the 250 publishing days available in a year, what does this mean for each book's chances of registering in the discourse? What does it mean that there was previously a system where the fixed price of a book applied to the first four years, while it today applies only to the first year? On the other hand, what does the introduction of barcodes on books, and of bonus systems in book stores mean for the availability of books? For example, when books were given barcodes, they could be sold in supermarkets, which in turn created new potentialities of distribution. Depending on the research needs, one may infinitely specify the materiality of text.

Furthermore, the archive as preconditions for action concerns systematic social access to and distribution of archive. And it is probably somewhere around here one shifts toward talking about a different materiality than text. This is likely to occur as we ask which parts of the archive are socially bound to which groups and institutions.

It might be helpful to reflect upon the distinctions between formal and informal organization. This distinction is often manifest in the social sciences, with one or the other prevailing within disciplinary methodological traditions. To illustrate: when was the last time you read a good social science discussion of an informal political organization?[5] And when did you read a good anthropological discussion of a formal political organization? Anthropologists almost exclusively study, for example, ethno-nationalism without regard for how states' formal organization establishes preconditions for ethno-politics. Discourse analysis seen as a method invites both these aspects—formal and informal—by broadly interrogating "preconditions for action."

It may also be methodologically useful to draw one last distinction, between institutions understood as regular patterns of interaction and institutions understood as physical infrastructure, precisely because it tends to disappear in language. Terms such as "the clinic," "the school," and "the military" are ambiguous in this respect. When their difference is announced through language, it happens so subtly that it rarely attracts explicit discussion. We rarely say that the school (the human collective consistent of teachers, cleaners, pupils, and so on) moves into a new school but rather into a new building (or, on the contrary, that pupils and teachers move into a new school). Furthermore, one may speak of going "to work," and intend a regular pattern of action, given that, for example, an academic may be at work in her office, her home, or in a seminar.

Emphasizing these distinctions leads to more precise questioning of the materiality of discourse: which linguistic and nonlinguistic preconditions for action are served by the relevant archive, and which formal and informal institutions (i.e., regular patterns of action) are activated?

To answer this, one may start by looking at Foucault's own practice. Here, we immediately encounter a problem, since Foucault, next to being a social scientist, was also a historian and a philosopher. He asks grandiose questions and answers them in equally sweeping terms. If one is interested in tectonic texts of grandiose scale, just go ahead. One may say something about difference and draw up a history about the present—a **genealogy**. The problem is that social science practice must also be able to capture social change at a smaller scale, and over shorter periods of time, than what such historical analyses aspire to. At least one and preferably several genealogies should ideally cover any given social phenomenon. But even where this is the case, there would still remain central questions. Discourse analysis must be more than genealogy, since it ought to apply to more diverse social practice. However, moving beyond genealogy implies magnifying the problem of materiality of discourse, since there is always a discourse that makes up preconditions for action, replete with material stasis. One cannot simply solve the research problem the way Foucault did, by tracing the genesis of materiality as a part of the genesis of discourse. Instead, one ought to objectify discourse, and adopt its materiality as a given assumption.

Box 5: Jens Bartelson, *A Genealogy of Sovereignty*

Jens Bartelson begins his *A Genealogy of Sovereignty* (1995) by apologizing for the difficult language, and with good reason. Reconceptualizing taken-for-granted stuff is always challenging, for it means wrestling with what has constituted oneself as a thinker.

The book presents a new conceptualization of sovereignty and a new reading of where it came from. Bartelson sees sovereignty as what frames politics, that is, something that sets politics off from other nonpolitical stuff and so delineates politics, but which is not itself either political or nonpolitical. Sovereignty frames politics, just like a frame (Gr. *parergon*) frames a picture. The modern way to do this, which followed different ways prevalent in what Bartelson calls the classical age and the Middle Ages respectively, was to invest sovereignty in the people of a state: the frame of politics equals the boundary of the nation-state—sovereignty is the state of having no one from outside dictate what happens inside of that boundary.

Methodologically, Bartelson's starting point is the Foucauldian observation that truth and knowledge are produced discursively, which is to say, in a social field where power is ever-present because it comes from everywhere. It follows that social phenomena like sovereignty are emergent, that is, they have no essence, but take their meaning from the ongoing contestation of how to fix the social phenomena's meaning. That the process is ongoing does not mean that it is continuous; new positions are built up over time and tend to assert their dominance swiftly, thus causing breaks in the meaning of concepts.

In order to bring out what the ontological status of a phenomenon thus understood is, Bartelson leans on a comparison of fire and sovereignty. Fire used to be treated, with air, water, and soil, as one of the basic four elements. When physics turned to understand the world in terms of molecules and thermodynamic laws, fire went up in smoke within scientific discourse. There was a break. In many other discourses, however, fire stayed on. The methodological lesson seems clear. Since phenomena have no essence, our job as analysts is to demonstrate how they are produced socially. We recognize de Saussure's understanding of language here: it is not the relationship between a concept and its reference (e.g., the word "fire" and the phenomenon fire) that is important but the relationship between different linguistically produced concepts of fire. So it is with sovereignty. Sovereignty cannot be boiled down to an "essence," legal or otherwise, for it only exists in its various incarnations in discourse. It follows that there is nothing to look for outside that discourse.

But isn't fire an apolitical term, and sovereignty a political one? In certain discourses, yes, but ask Buddhists in Tibet or fundamentalist Christian theologians who dwell on the nature of hell. To them, fire is deeply political. The methodological point here is simple: anything may become a political term, for drawing the distinction between what is political and what is not political is itself a political act (for example, in the 1970s Western feminist discourse spent enormous amounts of energy arguing that the private is political). Bartelson gives us a productive methodological chestnut when he suggests that the process just discussed may be understood in terms of asking three questions:

> If knowledge is understood as a system for the formation of valid statements, all knowledge is knowledge about differentiation, and this differentiation is a political activity. First, in order to constitute itself as such, some given knowledge must demarcate itself from what [. . .] is not knowledge, be it opinion, ideology or superstition. Second [. . .] knowledge implies a set of *ontological* decisions: what does exist, and what dos not exist [. . .] From these decisions, two other decisions follow. One is *ethical,* and tells us who we are, who is a friend, who is an enemy and who is a stranger. In short, the ethical decision is one of deciding who is Same and who is Other. The other decision is *metahistorical,* and tells us where *we* came from, how *we* became friends, how *we* got here, where *we* are, and where *we* are heading. In short, knowledge, being political to the extent that it differentiates, is indissolubly intertwined with identity and history. (Bartelson 1995: 6)

It follows that the questions to ask in order to understand a phenomenon like sovereignty include how an epoch defines knowledge versus nonknowledge (e.g., a god guarantees sovereignty), what exists (e.g., a people that may then be conceptualized as the keeper of sovereignty), who we are (e.g., subjects, citizens), and where we are in history (e.g., on our way to subjugate more territory to our sovereign rule). Such a genealogical undertaking, Bartelson stresses, cannot be causal (given the multi-causality involved in epochal shifts, that would be a tall order), but should rather be effective. By which he means that it should demonstrate how different logics succeed one another.

All this is very helpful methodologically—it helps the discursive analyst hook up to the world—but it does not tell us how to produce the data we need to demonstrate the shifts. Here, Bartelson stresses that both historical logics and historical shifts may be understood as episodes, and the analyst may nail episodes down in time by concentrating on the exemplary. One methodological challenge for the genealogist, writes Bartelson (1995: 55), is to avoid a "suprahistorical claim to truth or versimilitude." Since what must be studied are conceptualizations, and conceptualizations in the period studied played as a fight between texts, texts are what have to be studied. Here the challenge becomes which texts make for good examples? Bartelson's answer is that:

> An example is a good example to the extent that it can be multiplied, and a series of examples is a good series if the series displays a regularity beyond the individuality of each particular example. In short, an exemplary history is based on the possibility of finding general rules for particular cases, and particular cases for general rules. (Bartelson 1995: 8)

A series of examples cannot, therefore, exist only of canonical or traditionary texts, which Bartelson calls blueprints for reality (that is, the texts whose content proceeds to being replicated as social space), for what we need to know is exactly how these texts, which were by definition the ones that were consecrated as representative of the period, were actually *made to become* so central. In order to understand this becoming, this canonization of certain texts, we have to analyze the "silent murmur surrounding the history of canonical texts." That is, we need to interrogate the texts that Bartelson calls *manuals*, the ones that canonize the canonical texts. Hence, Bartelson's genealogy of sovereignty does not look at the established classics, but also at stuff that, for most other purposes, would be pretty obscure.

The problem is, then, not to move from a synchronic to a diachronic analysis. It emerges already when limiting the time period in question and studying a more specific text. An example is Edward Said's *Orientalism*, which we have referenced several times already. Said's work deals primarily with the 150 years prior to the time of its writing and focuses mostly on representations from the latter half on the 19th century. Said traces a discursive formation (Western thinking on the exotic) and investigates its material textuality (novels, historical works, paintings, and so on), its social practices (conferences, seminars), its formal institutions (university courses, colonial administrations), and its informal institutions (the networks connecting its practitioners, and their relation to its consumers). As noted earlier, Said rejected Foucault's assertion that the individual text or author counts for very little (1978: 23). We have arrived at a similar conclusion in our own research on "the East" that constitutes Europe and the imaginings of the Congo, respectively. In the cases we examined, we found materiality inviting a closer look at individual texts and even the role of their authors. Think for example of *Orientalism* as a text. Said portrayed many of his colleagues as orientalists. Several of these spent considerable energy in trying to create distance from the term. A Lebanese author replied that Said himself objectified the Occident: by insisting on a monolithic reading of "Western" discursive formation, Said's text became another carrier of the same discursive practices of "the West" as he accused his colleagues of doing to "the East." Said's work, moreover, inspired other researchers to deal with how Western academic and artistic representation of the Caribbean, India, Eastern Europe, and other regions objectified these places (Williams and Chrisman 1993; Wolff 1996; Neumann 1999).

The point here is that Said's text itself generated differences in the materiality of discourse—first of all by generating more text, but more importantly by altering the regularity of academic patterns of behavior. It is no coincidence that Said and another pioneer in these types of studies, Tzvetan Todorov (1984), are literary theorists. The reaction from social scientists was that this critique was, if not irrelevant, at least not meriting, as it was not pertaining to the discipline, and hence not a part of the scientific discourse. The book *Orientalism* and its phenomenal success in opening up a debate in many social sciences and area studies ultimately changed the standards for what was to be merited in academic hiring processes. Given that academic positions are launching pads for interventions in the general political debate, in which titles such as "professor," "researcher," and so on serve as labels that ease the access to media carrying the public debate, the book has also exerted some effect outside the scientific discourse, to the extent that regularity in patterns of behavior outside academia changed somewhat. If we draw on the distinctions above, it seems that the effect on some (but not all!) academic institutions was of a formal character, while the effects on other institutions were more informal.

The methodological problem is to specify this feedback loop. Considering that Orientalism is still present in academic and general public debate, it is unreasonable to speak of a shift in the discursive formation. But it is also unreasonable to speak of Orientalism as being as pervasive as it was 30 years ago.

Certainly, this problem is not new. It resembles recurrent questions, such as the extent to which Marx's writing changed history, Keynes's writing changed capitalism, and so on. Concerning Said's critique of Foucault for underestimating the chances that one text and one author have to influence discourse, it should also be acknowledged that Foucault's own practice might have been animated by a strategic intention to change contemporary social practices, and explicitly not meant as a study "for the record." What discourse analysis should be able to do with such questions is to move beyond studies of the author's intention, that is, what the author aimed at when she wrote, published, and marketed the text, and of accounts of reception in the form of reviews and overviews of debates, and focus instead on the materiality of reception, to readings of how institutional practice changes as a consequence of text presentation and reception. We believe it is crucial to specify the spatial factors here. In order to specify the relation between the debate and the materiality of discourse over short time periods, one better abandon the idea that specific texts and individuals are uninteresting. Such a view is fruitful when the historical sweep is substantial and covers sufficiently many discursive texts, but it turns into an unwarranted hurdle when studying more limited discursive formations over shorter periods of time.

Subject Positions and Institutions

Within sociology, the term "role" can be referred to as a set of norms, relations, and actions bound to a specific social context. Examples are "father," "discussant," "bureaucrat," and "tourist." The term "**subject position**" goes further. The idea is that discourse provides packages for how to live and behave not only in particular contexts but more generally. Subject positions are therefore typically more general than roles, such as "female Chinese university student" or "Latin American gay man."

Subject positions as they are shaped in discourse can serve as the basis for analysis. One might, however, also focus on the subject and its actions more directly. Bruno Latour (1986) is a protagonist of this approach. He insists that discourse is not an unconnected world but rather a population of players that mixes with things and society and sustains them. The entry point is thereby subjects and their positions vis-à-vis objects and institutions. Statements are the statements of subjects, and discourse can be considered a resource mobilization struggle between subjects. This poses a great opportunity for those interested in studying how entrepreneurs with political programs produce motivation and legitimacy. Such was the case in Kevin's work on the employment of autochthony discourses (e.g., claims to be privileged "sons of the soil") by political entrepreneurs in some contemporary African conflicts (Bøås and Dunn 2013). Politics can then be understood as explaining who people are in order to shape and re-represent the acting collective.

Such processes involve making a stream of diverse and surely internally contradictory events appear as ordered and relatively neutral—that is, to re-represent them in a way that aligns them to the stories that constitute the Self in question. Three events from World War II Denmark may serve as an example: When the country was invaded by Germany on April 8, 1940, international legal experts were mobilized to define the German intervention in a way that made state sovereignty appear nonbreached. When discovering that Danish Jews were to be deported to Germany, a network was mobilized to ship them off to neutral Sweden. During the war a good number of Danes volunteered to serve as Nazi soldiers on the East Front and were waved off by masses of people that showed up for their departure. After the war, there was a need for stories that addressed what the Danish Self really was, against which these and a number of other events seemed meaningful. In order to do so, these events had to be told in a particular way, or not told at all. A discourse analysis of these events could focus on the handful of Danish social democratic politicians, their advisors, their ties to historians and their control of archives, their allocations of funds to memorials, the honorable decorations, institutionalizing of bank holidays, and so forth. In other words, one could attempt an overview of those resources mobilized to tell homogenized stories about the Danish Self and those techniques applied to elevate these stories as more than competing stories, and preferably as the truth. One could assume that this would cover mobilization of the most diverse resources at hand.

Latour and similar scholars are interested in how specific subjects create new meaning, new subject positions, new types of action, new items. In particular within postcolonial studies and feminist theory, such scholars have additionally been interested in how persons or collectives relate to discursive formations that offer them second-class subject positions (a term often used within postcolonial theory is "subaltern"; see for example Spivak 1987). While Said, an important but controversial source of inspiration, emphasized the importance of discourse and left the colonized subjects appearing as completely overrun, or better, as astute but intoxicated by discourse, the point here is rather to unravel political strategies that may empower subjects. As Sue Mills puts it in a discussion of feminism and discourse analysis:

> individual subjects should not be seen simply to adopt roles which are mapped out for them by discourses; rather, they experience discomfort with certain elements implicit in discourses, they find pleasure in some elements, they are openly critical about others. Individual subjects are constantly weighing up their own perception of their own position in relation to these discursive norms against what they assume other individuals or groups perceive their position to be. In this way, the process of finding a position for oneself within discourse is never fully achieved. (1997: 97)

A different way of approaching discourse analysis is by focusing on an institution and then tracing the subject positions it produces. "Institution" can be understood as both formal and informal, but it concerns regularized patterns of behavior and not physical infrastructure. If the basis of analysis is an institution, there is no problem to also see it in its aspect as physical infrastructure. There exist for example many discourse analyses of companies that seek to demonstrate how these companies generate specific subject positions. It is again evident how this differs from Foucault's discourse analyses, in which the point was to study the emergence of both institutions and subject positions, for example, the prison and the criminal. Foucault's framework becomes too crude for those with more delicate research needs. It is symptomatic to see how Foucault generalizes on institutions' delineation of expressions through three mechanisms: first, through prohibitions or taboos (formal or informal denial); second, by categorizing a set of possible statements in a way that renders those who utter them unreliable and therefore mad, so that the statements become materialized madness; and third, by questioning whether statements are truthful or not (Foucault 1981). If the starting point for the analysis is a specific organization (which instantiates forms of organizations or institutions of the overarching type that Foucault is interested in) there is a need for a more finely knit approach.

Let's take Caroline Casey's (1995) study of a US-based transnational hi-tech company as an example. In terms of method, it is interesting to note how Casey has used participatory observations in addition to text studies as data for her discourse analysis. Casey argues that the shift from the industrial to the postindustrial society is characterized by a shift from bureaucratic rationality to "designer capitalism." Production in the old industrial society was divided so that each occupation had its specific tasks. Subject positions were then primarily connected to professional education and belonging. In the time of designer capitalism, however, it is no longer the occupations that form the building blocks of production processes. Instead, it is what Casey calls "discursive means of production," and these can be acquired in many different ways. A set of subject positions thereby diminish in importance, while the new ones are less significant: "replacing occupation as a primary locus of class and self-identification in the corporate workplace is team and knowledge [. . . .] Relationship to a product, to team-family members and to the company displaces identification with occupation and its historic repository of skills, knowledges and allegiances" (Casey 1995: 109). The result for the individual is what she calls a "colluded self," with a tendency to narcissism, which is "dependent, over-agreeable, compulsive in dedication and diligence, passionate about the product and the company. The colluded self is comforted by primary narcissistic gratifications of identification with a workplace family free of the older attractions of occupation- and class-based solidarities" (Casey 1995: 191). Designer capitalism has created its designer employees.

Paul du Gay's study of four sales firms also assumes a shift away from bureaucratic rationality toward more indirect governance, in which management emphasizes the employees' internalization of techniques useful to optimize market adaptability. The result is what du Gay calls "enterprising selves," continuously engaged in a reflexive adaptation and optimization of work (1996: 56–64). The reason for du Gay to emphasize the self-controlling reflexive aspect where Casey instead emphasizes team spirit is probably due to differences in the institutional function under scrutiny: while the main undertaking in a hi-tech company is still to produce a certain product, the prime preoccupation of the sales businesses is to manage the relation with the market.

Box 6: Paul Willis, *Learning to Labour*

Mention should be made of a kind of social analysis that emerged in the Anglo-American world in parallel to, but at first mutually unacknowledged by, discourse analysis. This is the work emerging from the Centre for Contemporary Cultural Studies at Birmingham University, better known as the Birmingham School of Cultural Studies. This work is post-Marxist in the same general way as is discourse analysis: the starting point is Marxist understandings of capitalist class societies, and the break with Marxism concerns impatience with the deterministic character of Marxism. Discourse analysts reacted against Levi-Straussian and Marxist structuralisms by swapping the idea of a latent structure underlying society at large with the idea of discourse as a more local and malleable system for forming utterances. The Birmingham School reacted against Marxist structuralism by looking not at how the organization of material production (what Marxists call *base*) reproduces social structures but rather at how culture (what Marxists call *superstructure*) reproduces social relations. In both cases, there is a move away from abstract analysis of social forces in general toward attention to the specific practices (including talk) of specific people, what makes it possible for them to act in these ways and what effects it has that they do.

The Birmingham School focused on what discourse analysts call subaltern groups, namely ethnic minorities, sexual minorities, and marginalized groups such as young white working-class males. Our example is a study of an English group of the latter, so-called lads. In *Learning to Labour: How Working Class Kids Get Working Class Jobs* (1977), Paul Willis followed a group of lads through their last year of school and into their six months of work. He charts their way of life, "laddism," ethnographically. Laddism is about thwarting authority, by not taking orders, by not paying attention in class or doing home-work, by being insubordinate, by staking out an alternative way of being in the world centered on dressing differently, thieving, and smoking. In middle-class families, these attitudes will find a counter-weight at home, but in working-class families, they will be considered normal. Fathers will recognize what Scott (1985) later called the "weapons of the weak" from their own shop floor working lives and underwrite the general behaviors on display. The lads will have their sights firmly placed on what they consider real life—drinking, going with girls, having a laugh—and will regard schooling as an irrelevant activity toward scoring in those areas. Once the lads enter working life, which, crucially, happens in all kinds of fortuitous ways, since work is thought of as generalized labor that is, once again, a diversion from the major focus of having a good time, they will earn their first money. They will marry and have children. At this point, there is no escape from working life, for without school credentials, they cannot go beyond generalized labor, and with families, they cannot afford taking time out to qualify for skilled work. As Willis puts it,

> The astonishing thing which this book attempts to present is that there is a moment—and it only needs to be this for the gates to shut on the future—in working class culture when the manual giving of labour power represents both a freedom, election and transcendence, and a precise insertion into a sys-

tem of exploitation and oppression for working people. The former promises the future, the latter shows the present. (1977: 120)

The point is that there is no need to pose any kind of materialist determinism, let alone any sinister class-hegemonic conspiracy on the part of the upper classes, to explain why lads let themselves remain working class, as he puts it. It is enough to demonstrate how these boys reproduce their fathers' lives and working nonchoices by documenting and analyzing their chosen opposition to a schooling system that is experienced as culturally alien because it is differently classed. Foucault once stated that we are trapped inside a prison of our own making, by which he meant that it is the cumulative sum of culturally specific practices, and not some outside force, that limits our scope for being in the world. Willis concurs and brilliantly demonstrates how this happens in one specific setting—a late-modern industrial town in the English Midlands—to one group of people—oppositional white teenage boys.

As we read it today, the book has some obvious weaknesses. While the parents are treated relationally—that is, Willis deals with the formation of the children as an outcome of their relations with their parents—the teachers are treated confrontationally—that is, simply as seen one-dimensionally by the lads. This is standpoint scholarship, in which the perspective is driven by identification with the group studied, rather than analytical scholarship, where the major interest concerns understanding the social form as such. Discourse analysis, whose main focus is what makes certain patterns possible, is of the analytical kind, not of the standpoint kind. As its impact grew within British academia from the late 1970s onward, however, many later works by Birmingham School scholars gravitated closer to discourse analysis.

These discourse analyses make an interesting turn. Instead of making text the basis and working their way toward the sociocultural, as Fairclough does, they start by looking directly at the tangible institution.

Casey even starts by postulating that the materiality in question is discursive. Contrary to Foucault, who still imagines that a set of societal, institutional, and economic "primary relations" is attached to production, Casey fuses this perspective and the discursive. Materiality is both specific (instantiated) in the enterprises she studies and produces subject positions with sufficient similarities for her to refer to "designer employees."

If we think about these different techniques as a whole, the conclusion is that they all "solve" the materiality of discourse problem by objectifying a part of the social, and observe how the other aspects of the social are influenced by or influences the objectified part. Humans act; they do so within a set of predefined social categories; and the categories are as a consequence confirmed, adjusted, or disabled based on human action. To specify this process has been a main preoccupation of social science since its dawn. No social theory has so far arrived at a satisfying response to how it all works out. One is left with trying out existing bits of the puzzle on new empirical research and coming up with new suggestions of how to solve it.

SUGGESTED FURTHER READINGS

Dunn, Kevin. 2003. *Imagining the Congo*. New York: Palgrave.

Lincoln, Bruce. 1989. *Discourse and the Construction of Society: Comparative Studies of Myth, Ritual and Classification*. Oxford: Oxford University Press.

Neumann, Iver B. 2012. *At Home with the Diplomats: Inside a European Foreign Ministry*. Ithaca: Cornell University Press.

Said, Edward. 1978. *Orientalism*. Harmondsworth, UK: Penguin.

Shepherd, Laura. 2008. *Gender, Violence and Security*. London: Zed Books.

4 | Getting Started

This chapter covers the preliminary steps needed for successfully conducting discourse analysis. We present some observations about prerequisites before exploring how one conceives of a research question from the perspective of conducting discourse analysis. By drawing upon our own scholarship and other examples of discourses analysis in the social sciences, we explore how one identifies and categorizes various sources of "data." We pay particular attention to concerns about how one chooses texts for analysis, how to delimit the scope of one's research, as well as questions related to different types of texts. We conclude with a few reflections on when the discourse analyst decides that she has enough research material.

Prerequisites

Perhaps the primary prerequisite to conducting most forms of social research is acquiring a certain degree of cultural competence. This is particularly true for discourse analysis, given that discourses are "grids of intelligibility" that are frequently quite culturally specific.

It may be useful to draw on extant knowledge when choosing a topic. It saves time, and you can start out with a competitive advantage. It also ensures a certain degree of cultural competence. For example, Iver did his conscription at the Norwegian Army Language School, where he studied Russian. He then lived in Russia for half a year and went on to take university courses in its history and foreign policy. All this gave him a certain cultural competence when he set out to research Soviet discourse as a doctoral student (later published as Neumann 1996). He knew the Russian language, genres of relevant texts, and something about the general social and political setting (such as when Russia was at war with other states that it considered to be European and the extent to which European history and language were taught in Russian schools). For his recent scholarly work, Kevin has been writing on punk rock culture around the globe (Dunn forthcoming). He has been able to draw upon almost three decades of active involvement in a number of punk communities, providing him with a useful level of cultural competency. But his research has also led him to conduct field research on four different continents. While his command of, say, the Indonesian language is nonexistent, Kevin's cultural competency around global punk (for example, his familiarity with bands in Jakarta) has been invaluable for his research and provided him entrée into communities and conversations that he otherwise would not have had access to.

For both of us, these examples of cultural competence enabled us to use tools of discourse analysis to demonstrate variations in meanings and representations. The more in-depth the general knowledge, the easier the specific research. For example, Iver knew that many Soviet newspaper articles were divided into two parts: a first part that repeated the so-called main line, then a part that dealt with new material that still had not been sorted in relation to and assimilated by that dominant representation. What is crucial for the discourse analyst is the separation of these two parts by *one* code word, *odnako*, which is best translated as "however." If one knows such conventions, the reading of texts becomes easier: Iver could rush through part one, which is a simple re-presentation of an already known reality, and concentrate on part two. Similarly, as Kevin read through Riot Grrrl zines, he was able to understand cultural references (e.g., "sXe" or "queercore")[1] and the rather specialized language of a music-based subculture that would at least at first have been impenetrable to outsiders.

Of course, some things may be learned on the job. As a British-trained Norwegian Russian specialist, Iver needed to work at mastering phrases like "to go" and "drag it through the garden" to buy a hamburger in the United States. Likewise, in Kevin's work on Belgian representations of the Congo, there were historic and/or cultural references that local friends in

Brussels had to help him with. When Iver turned to the analysis of discourse in the United States, he had to get acquainted with ubiquitous references such as "I have a dream" (a speech by Martin Luther King, Jr.), "beam me up, Scotty" (a line from the television show *Star Trek*), or "I pledge allegiance" (to the flag, something that is done every day in every school of the country). The point is that a researcher needs a basic level of cultural competence to recognize the shared understandings that create a common frame of reference, which makes it possible for people to act in relation to one another.

There is a trade-off with cultural competence. Culture appears to be shared. Close up, it turns out not to be (Frykman and Løfgren 2003). Phrases may mean a number of different things, or they may be used without the user knowing all their cultural references or implications. The challenge for the researcher is not to get naturalized—not to "become" part of the universe studied—but to maintain the ability to denaturalize. If you are a native speaker and know a culture as only a native can, then you may struggle to obtain that marginal gaze where things look strange enough to present themselves as puzzles. You will also lose touch with your own biases. You become what anthropologists call "home blind." This has been an ongoing struggle in Kevin's attempt to write about punk culture, given that he remains an active participant in that culture. It is fully possible to do discourse analysis in the culture you know best, but you still need some kind of distance. You cannot be *too much* at home.

At this point, an astute historian or anthropologist would ask: whose representations, whose culture? We are talking about cultural competence regarding the culture that spawns the representations to be analyzed, not necessarily for other related cultures. When Iver completed his discourse analysis of Russian representations of Europe, he noted that he had documented what he considered to be so much arcane and downright silly Russian representations of Europe that he felt he owed it to Russians to analyze European representations of Russia as well, presuming that just as much arcane and silly stuff would crop up (it did; see Neumann 1999). For that analysis of European representations of Russia, Iver needed neither Russian nor much knowledge of Russia. Instead, it was important to know German, French, and English. It was a problem that Iver could only cover

Spanish and Portuguese representations in translations. But he still felt warranted in talking about *European* representations of Russia, for there were strong regularities between German, British, French, and Scandinavian representations of Russia at any one given time during the last 500 years. Since Iberia was in the same cultural ambit, some sameness could be assumed. That said, there is no substitute for doing proper studies of Iberian representations, first, to ascertain the regularity in European representations, and second, to find out if there are special features or indeed entirely different representations in evidence.

As in any other research, this lacuna has to be stated, and it will serve as a challenge to new researchers. Methodologically, this points to the importance of being explicit about your sweep: the broader it is, the more general knowledge you need, and the less risky it is to leave lacunae. But great care should be taken here. No good Russianist would assume cultural competence about Serbia, and old cultural competence from the Soviet era may not necessarily be applied uncritically to Ukraine after its formal political separation from Russia. Knowing the ever-changing limits of your cultural competence may be as important as knowing its contents.

Conceiving a Research Question

As all the factors that social science research examines—be they biological, psychological, institutional—are, first and foremost, discursive objects, one could apply discourse analysis to almost any research question. But, depending upon your ontological and epistemological proclivities, discourse analysis might not be the ideal method to use. We suggest that you have another look at chapter 1 to ensure that this approach, as opposed to other social science approaches, is the right one for you and your research. Assuming that it is, we suggest that the next step is to establish some parameters for completing a successful project.

It is always useful to reflect on exactly what is animating your curiosity regarding a certain subject. What aspects of the puzzle are grabbing your attention? What are the issues, events, or phenomena that you feel you absolutely must know more about or understand better? This might not always be self-evident, especially as we sometimes suppress what we want to explore in favor of what we think we *ought* to explore. And while it is useful to have a research question driven by intellectual curiosity and passion, that passion should also be commensurate with the duration of the time allowed for the project. After all, a semester-long research project is quite different than a doctoral thesis. Articulating a list of specific research questions can be useful, especially if you are able to cluster certain questions together and to organize them into subquestions. This provides a discernible landscape for the potential research project, helping to clarify in which directions your curiosity and interests might be driving you.

There is, ultimately, almost always an arbitrary element in case selection. Many cases may actually work just as well as the ones you end up choosing. It is always useful to keep in mind that your project should be personally relevant and enjoyable, as well as doable. Simple logistical issues will always determine some parameters of your research. For example, basic language limitations matter: if you don't speak or read the language that most of the data is in, you should probably find another case. Or there simply might not be enough information for discourse analysis to be a viable choice—one needs a critical mass of text in order to ascertain what the representations are. For instance, Luis Lobo-Guerrero's genealogical work on the relationship between security and risk through its materialization in insurance was greatly shaped by what he found (and didn't find) in archives (2013: 123). He found he had to be flexible in adapting his research project based on the limitations of the archives. Of course, life intervenes as well. Roxanne Doty's *Imperial Encounters* (1996) relied upon archival sources partly because she conducted her research when she was pregnant and then raising her young daughter alone, thus limiting her ability to conduct extensive fieldwork. Likewise, Kevin was set to conduct fieldwork in the Congo (then called Zaïre) when the country quickly collapsed into a civil war, throwing his research plans (and funding sources) into disarray. The archives proved to be a rewarding place of internal exile. Regardless of the choices you make (or are made for you), as a good researcher you should be honest about them and their implications on your research (see Neumann and Neumann 2015).

It is easy to get overwhelmed by a topic that is just too unwieldy. It may be useful to pick a very narrow, specific topic that allows you to explore much larger issues. After having to scrap his plans for extensive fieldwork in the Congo, Kevin chose to examine how the Congo had been represented within the international community, beginning with its colonial conquest up to the current civil war. This case study led him to explore not only issues of colonialism and neocolonialism but also the social construction of sovereignty, the performativity of stateness, repression and resistance, and the decline of the Westphalian state system. However, telling the definitive story of how the Congo has been imagined over the past century would be an overwhelming task, filling numerous volumes. To make his project doable, he focused on four historical moments: the colonial "invention" of the Congo at the end of the nineteenth century; its decolonization in 1960; its reinvention as "Zaïre" during the 1970s; and the "return" of the Congo at the end of the twentieth century. During each of these four periods, the identity of the Congo was being contested, with numerous forces attempting to produce and attach meanings to its territory and people. These forces sought to create "regimes of truth" about the Congo by defining and inscribing its identity.

Kevin originally wanted to have six historical moments but found that would require more time and effort than was reasonable. When choosing the historical moments to focus on, he had to make clear intellectual justifications for each. He had long been fascinated by the 1974 Ali-Foreman "Rumble in the Jungle" boxing match and realized that this actually represented an important moment in the marketing of the Congo as "Zaïre" to the international community. But if there had not been a larger justification for examining this moment, the fight simply being an interesting event would not have been enough to warrant its inclusion in the study. When examining discourses from a historical perspective, one measure for selecting points is to focus on when forces were seeking to create regimes of truth about the object of inquiry by defining and inscribing its meaning. This type of approach stresses historical contingency with a focus on ruptures and disjunctures rather than continuities. As we will discuss in the next chapter, one could also focus on these continuities.

Finally, we think that it is useful to explicitly construct your research question to reflect the "how-possible" framing within discourse analysis. This move goes back to our discussion in chapter 2 concerning how discourse analysis is different from other approaches in the social sciences. Other approaches tend to frame research questions in terms of "why"— presupposing identities and meanings within the social realm. As Doty notes, "Why questions generally take as unproblematic the *possibility* that particular policies and practices could happen. . . . In contrast, how questions examine how meanings are produced and attached to various social subjects and objects, thus constituting particular interpretive dispositions that create certain possibilities and preclude others" (1996: 4; emphasis in original). We believe that framing research questions in terms of "how-possible" makes explicit the critical interrogation of discourses necessary for successful analysis.

Box 7: Roxanne Doty, *Imperial Encounters*

Roxanne Doty's 1996 monograph critically explores two "imperial encounters": one between the United States and the Philippines, the other between Great Britain and Kenya. She examines these two encounters in parallel: beginning with the establishment of a colonial relationship; the development of counterinsurgency policies to put down armed resistance in both colonies; and contemporary relations around foreign aid, democracy, and human rights. Like Edward Said, Doty is interested in examining the ways in which "the South has been discursively represented by policy makers, scholars, journalists, and others in the North" (1996: 2). The starting point is that foreign policy is a discursive practice where a certain Self, for example, a state, represents Others in certain ways. This process, called Othering, fixes the identity of the Self by delineating the self from other agents. This delineation creates or is constitutive of the self, for with another delineation the self would have been different. This is what poststructuralists mean when they talk about others as a *constitutive outside* for the self. Central to Doty's analysis are the connections between discourse and practice. As she writes, "the term *imperial encounters* is meant to convey the idea of asymmetrical encounters in this one entity has been able to construct 'realities' that were taken seriously and acted upon and the other entity has been denied equal degrees of kinds of agency" (1996: 3).

Building upon Laclau and Mouffe's understanding of discourse, Doty examines how discourses work to produce knowledge that appears as "natural." To do so, she specifies the different types of "work" accomplished within discourses. For Doty, discourses naturalize through the establishment of background knowledge that is taken to be true (presupposition), as well as through the construction of classificatory schemes that produce "natural" hierarchies. Within discourses, Doty tracks the rhetorical strategies utilized, particularly the process of negation and positioning of subjects and objects vis-à-vis one another (which tend to follow either the logic of difference or the logic of equivalence). In her work, Doty utilizes discourse analysis in a close, critical reading of legislative debates, reports of colonial administrations, media reports, and academic treatises. Some critics noted that Doty's approach could have been strengthened by working with a wider range of primary sources, such as music, literature, cartoons, maps, and other alternative "texts." Regardless, Doty's work represented an important intervention for discourses analysts in Western political science and international relations scholarship.

Identifying and Selecting Sources

As one moves from conceiving a research question to designing the research project, one must consider what type of texts or "data" to study. To be rather simplistic, discourse analysts treat discourses as the "data" to be analyzed. Specifically, because discourse analysis entails an examination of texts (both linguistic and nonlinguistic), we can understand texts as a form of "data." The smallest unit of study is the utterance. Utterances are often textual, but they may also be visual or any other form of semiotic data. For example, Iver has carried out a discourse analysis of monuments that constitute group identity; in this case, the utterances are things like Egyptian inscriptions on temple walls, Greek vases, churches, statues. Ultimately, the choice of data should be structured according to the research question posed and the researcher's ontological and epistemological assumptions. But, as noted earlier, it may also be shaped by necessity and accessibility.

Choosing Texts

In earlier chapters, we presented the speech by JFK on juvenile delinquency as a useful example for discourse analysis. But it is important to note that it is simply one data point and ultimately does not tell us enough about the relevant discourses at play. Discourse analysis usually requires employing multiple texts because, as Milliken argues, "a single source cannot be claimed to support empirical arguments about discourse as a social background" (1999: 233). Our focus is on those discursive formations that enable texts and binds them together. But what then is the status of an individual text? Several discourse analysts have grappled with this problem. As we noted earlier, Foucault asserted that the individual text or author counts for very little, but Edward Said argued, "I do believe in the determining imprint of individual writers upon the otherwise anonymous collective body of texts constituting a discursive formation like Orientalism" (1978: 23).

Our own discourse analyses often go in the same direction: a few texts written by a few individuals seem to be important. There are obviously several preconditions that enable certain texts to find a broad audience, such as Harriet Beecher Stowe's *Uncle Tom's Cabin*, Joseph Conrad's *Heart of Darkness,* or Samuel Huntington's article on "The Clash of Civilizations." Often, they are characterized by linking and sharpening a number of loosely knitted assumptions already present in discourse, and are supported by moral and institutional resources. But methodically there is another important point here: resistance to reality is possible. Certain texts undermine social reality. Such texts might just short-circuit the closed feedback-loop between reality, moral values, and institutions. We will return to this point below.

For now, we need to address a key question: if discourse analysts read texts, how do they determine which texts? In certain cases this is a simple question to answer. If one is to study party systems, then party programs, election laws, and articles, as well as speeches by party leaders are typical primary materials. Still, the quantity of material is usually enormous, especially if one includes the secondary literature. It is crucial to draw some lines, but there are always inherent problems associated with the process of delimitation (e.g., where does one erect boundaries, what is lost through exclusion, etc.). Ultimately, the choices need to be justified and the process retraceable. As Mutlu and Salter argue, "Good discourse analysis will also identify what the meaning is of the data collected through formal content analysis that measures: the appearance or dominance of a particular phrase or set of terms; the persistence of a metaphorical trope such as inside/outside, Self/Other, national security/international anarchy; or the development of a linguistic or visual practice" (2013: 116).

A given discourse cannot be entirely detached from all other discourses. They are ordered and scaled in relation to one another. For example, if one repeatedly finds European statements such as "scrape a Russian and the Tatar will appear" (as Iver did), it would be mistaken to omit representations of Tatars from an analysis of European representations of Russian identity. Russian identity, therefore, must be studied as something Russian and something non-Russian. However, which relation or relations to study—between Russia and Asia, Russia and Europe, Russia and Germany, Russia and Tatarstan, Russia and the Jews, Russia and the feminine—is not given. Ideally, all should be covered. In practice, that is rarely possible. The choice of which relation(s) to single out may be theory driven (e.g., let us see what happens if we bring a feminist standpoint perspective to the study of Russian identity and look at the constitutive role of gender), utilitarian (e.g., I need to illuminate the identity aspects involved before I can get a handle on Russian-German energy relations; how do Russians think of Germany in general?), or ludic (in Iver's case: why is it that Russians treat me the way they do? This must have something to do with general Russian ideas about Europeans).

Insofar as politics is a struggle between named groups and people, politics is conflict. Conflict should therefore attract the analyst of political discourse. One will often find direct references in a text to other texts that are being attacked. It is usually apparent who is attacking whom. When there is such a racket, it is because something new is happening, something that is meeting various attempts at limitation from those who dominate the discourse (Lukes 1974). However, the pursuit of commotion can be a methodological problem, since realities are maintained by the frequent repetition and confirmation of representations. The absence of commotion does not mean that the discourse in question is nonconflictual. One has to use more time and mental energy to work out how and why things remain unaltered. Concentrating on the texts that produce the greatest racket might mean that one automatically privileges the dominant representation, which usually will be the loudest (Wæver 1999). Some texts remain unpublished when censorship is successful. Challengers may remain undetected for other reasons, including socially distributed lack of writing skills. One may also turn this around: publications that only repeat or incrementally expand the main representation tend to pass relatively quietly. If one fails to detect these processes of power, then the analysis easily becomes a shallow one of the boundaries of the discourse and its domination.

Social and political life is full of cases where somebody writes something new and intriguing, with no immediate reception whatsoever. It may simply be that the text is so new or different in relation to what already exists that it goes unnoticed for this very reason. There are existing texts as well as future texts that will suffer this fate. If a text from a relatively obscure source becomes central—as did Francis Fukuyama's "The End of History?" in *The National Interest* (1989)—then it is a research task to demonstrate how the text overcame the odds inculcated by its lowly publishing origins.

Some texts will show up as crossroads or anchor points, such as short government treatises outlining policy (called white papers in most English-speaking countries). These are called **canonical texts** or **monuments** (compare Laclau and Mouffe 2001 [1985] on **nodal points**). In both of our dissertation research (dealing with quite different topics), we each were largely able to identify textual canon by starting with the secondary literature, because it proved to be well-informed. We both took as "monuments" the works that were generally cited in the secondary literature (whether it was Henry Morten Stanley's travelogues in the Congo and

Conrad's *Heart of Darkness* or 1840s writings by Russians Slavophiles and Westernizers). In both of our cases, we read what we considered to be the monumental works on the topic and found that they tended to refer to one another. This, as well as the negative finding that there were few additional central texts, confirmed them as monuments.

It is useful to select texts around these monuments, since monuments also contain references to other texts, which again pointed us to others that were related. One discovers that some texts are "canonical," in the sense that they have a broad reception and are often cited. If one identifies these texts, reads them, and then reads the central texts that these texts in turn refer to, soon one is able to identify the main positions and versions. In most contemporary Western nationality discourses, for example, the representation of history for political purposes is widespread.

Delimiting Your Scope

However, it is not always possible to go back to antediluvian events, so one must delimit the timeframe. We've already mentioned Kevin's decision to focus his examination of four "ruptures" in the history of Congolese representation. In Iver's case, once he had chosen his dissertation topic, he read up on the secondary literature in order to identify cutoff points. An obvious one would have been the coming to power of the great Europeanizer Peter the Great in 1694. In order to trace discourse in more depth, he chose the Napoleonic wars that really brought Russia into the heart of European great power politics, and treated the period from 1694 to 1815 cursorily as a prehistory. The other cutoff point presented itself during the work, as the Soviet Union split up in the autumn of 1991.

In specifying the sweep of the analysis, it is also important to keep in mind your reader. Iver later did a discourse analysis on Norwegian representations of Europe (Neumann 2001). He tried to tackle the question of home blindness by going way back in time (after all, who is really "at home" in the Middle Ages?). In this case, the main intended reader was an informed Norwegian. He therefore needed to be fairly detailed in drawing up representations from the last 50 years. Yet he did not present context that was already fairly well-known, which would not be particularly interesting to the prospective reader. When he did a shorter version in English (Neumann 2002b), the intended readers were different, so he dropped detail and filled in context. Likewise, Kevin's writing on global punk has been published for both academic and punk audiences, and he has made decisions accordingly, not just about tone but also presentation of background knowledge and the level of necessary discursive explanation.

A doctoral student in Europe, who has little idea who his readers will be, will tend to write differently from an American student, who has a committee from the outset. And how do you weigh writing for your examiners against writing for a more general audience that may also be interested in the texts? There are authorial decisions to be made—different strokes for different folks; broader ones for nonspecialist foreigners, dense teachers and/or colleagues, and academics working in outer disciplines. We suggest that you be cognizant of the decisions you are making and, when appropriate, provide justifications for them.

Participants themselves also delimit their discourses. For example, medical diagnosis relies upon the definition of diseases and syndromes, upon which doctors draw. Analyzing the struggles over these definitions, and the process of getting them registered as such, form part of the research. If the chosen discourse is *international* intervention (to distinguish from medical interventions), then the struggle over the characterization of certain policies as "humanitarian" is decisive. The main task is to dig out the production of specialized knowledge. In analyzing German human rights law, for example, there will be a number of relevant texts in legal journals and government policy papers. One can compare related professional discourses in other countries. However, the connection to general political discourse may not be explicit.

Some texts can acquire importance from the medium through which they are delivered. For example, the newly elected prime minister of the Congo, Patrice Lumumba, delivered the 1960 Independence Day speech that was broadcast throughout the country via radio. It was also reproduced in newspapers and pamphlets in the Congo and across much of Europe, giving him an international audience unimagined by any Congolese individual beforehand. His challenges to the accepted Belgian narrative of colonization were powerful not just because of his eloquence but because of the speech's global circulation. In the same vein, a private letter from the 1830s threatened the dominant Russian representation of Europe after it got a wide reception through the circulation of copies in the saloons of St. Petersburg (the author was declared mentally ill and incarcerated). It is important to bear in mind the values that different media give texts. If one is to carry out a discourse analysis of peace operations in the 2010s, it is important to distinguish between those journals that aim at operative milieus (*Foreign Affairs* or *Survival*), those that are written for a more general audience (*International Affairs* in Europe), and those that are mainly read by academics (*International Peacekeeping*).

But what of those speeches given by Congolese independence activists unheard beyond the individuals in the audience or, for that matter, of an unpublished Russian manuscript from the 1930s, unseen by more than a handful of people? In terms of the history of ideas, these examples would be very interesting, precisely because of their originality and their lack of reception. Their discovery would provide a more accurate definition of the borderline between possible thought and the communication of that possibility. In terms of Congolese independence or the European politics in the 1930s, however, they would be interesting only in the degree that they spawned other, socially communicated texts.

What if it turns out that there are a number of texts that are systematically overlooked, which jointly document that there was a main representation that previously had not been included in the analysis? In the area of women and war, one can at least imagine the possibility that a systematic reading of all available sources on US national service in 1917 written by women would result in a revision of previous views of the national service institution. Mikhail Bakhtin's (1986) concept of **genre** is useful here, for genre carries its own memory, in the sense that every text relies on its predecessors and carries with it their echoes. If previous analysts have for some reason overlooked an entire genre, then it is an important research task to cast light upon how this has happened. This will change the way we remember a given historical sequence and is politically relevant to today's situation. Excavate one text on women and war, and you have an idiosyncratic voice and an indication that a group has not met the preconditions for action to make itself heard. Excavate many, and you have documentation that an entire group has been silenced. It is also possible that there are too few texts published, making it difficult to get started. One can carry out a discourse analysis of material that has not been in general circulation (for example, of classified material). If the reason for the lack of text is the novelty of the specific discourse, with, for example, only newspaper articles existing, it is possible to include a small text-based analysis of this material in an analysis that also draws upon other methods of data collection, for example, interview surveys or participant observation.

There are also strong theoretical reasons to supplement text-based discourse analysis with other methods of data collection. In *The Politics of Insecurity* (2006), Jef Huysmans expresses concern that discursive approaches tend to privilege and prioritize political speeches and writings. His concern is that this practice results in an implicit bias in the direction of focusing on professional politicians and opinion makers (2006: 8). In his work, Huysmans also employs a practice-driven approach that engages in the "technologies of government," such as the issuing of passports, visas, and so forth, to explore the intersection of migration and asylum with discourses of fear and security in the European Union.

At the same time, there are reasons why many discourse analysts have privileged "official" discourses. As Lene Hansen (2006: 7) has argued, policymakers are situated within the larger political and public sphere, which means that their representations draw upon and are formed by the representations articulated by a large number of individuals, institutions, and media outlets. Thus, policymakers are significant conveyers of the basic discourses at play. Yet there is a concern that a distinction between "official" and "popular" discourses may be partly a fiction, a product of power that is reified by academic disciplines. We have both produced works, for instance, that challenge the tradition within political science of privileging government documents, speeches by state leaders, the writings of political elites, and similar "legitimate" sources of data within the discipline. There is extra value to be had from engaging nontraditional data, particularly popular literature, movies, television shows, music, cartoons, and so forth. This raises issues regarding employing a broad reach when collecting data, as well as organizing (and possibly weighing) types of discursive data.

Variations in the Types of Texts

In *Writing the War on Terrorism* (2005), Richard Jackson sought to examine the way in which official and public language was deployed by the George W. Bush administration to mobilize and justify its global campaign of counterterrorism. To do so, Jackson chose to engage with a wide array of discursive sources, ultimately resulting in the establishment of a four-tiered pyramid of source material. The first tier included the "whole corpus of official speeches, media interviews, press releases, radio and television addresses and articles written by leading figures in the administration" (2005: 17). The second tier consisted of laws, policy documents, national strategy statements, and official reports. The third set included internal memos and reports, emails and letters, operational manuals, briefing papers, and the established rules and standard operating procedures of all agencies and institutions involved in the counterterrorism campaign. The fourth tier consisted of all symbolic and emblematic representations employed (2005: 17–18). Thus, Jackson systematically constructed a clearly delineated data set for his discourse analysis.

When researching the construction of Congolese identity, Kevin also engaged empirical data from a broad array of sources, but in a much less systematic way. While the majority came from the "official" realm of governmental reports, speeches, and documents, he also drew from journalism, travel literature, academic treatises, fiction, film, museum displays, art, images, maps, and other "popular" texts. His argument was that these texts often provide the most vivid and potent examples of the techniques through which Third World subjects have been narrated by Western hegemonic powers. For many outside observers, including politicians, these are the sources that have provided the primary framework within which the Congo has been made "knowable." As the historian David Newbury (1998) pointed out, many Westerners are intellectually uninformed about the Congo but are so inundated by stereotypical images that they feel they have a well-defined cognitive framework. In his preliminary research, Kevin came to understand that novels such as *Heart of Darkness*, films such as *Tarzan*, and cartoons such as *Tintin in the Congo* contributed to the basic discursive structure through which many Westerners viewed the

Congo, even today. Thus, he believed it was important to cast the net wide when constructing his data set.

Exploring the ruptures around the discursive production of the Congo also drove Kevin to engage with a wide and diverse spectrum of sources and authors. During the 1960s, for instance, the identity of the Congo was contested on the floor of the UN General Assembly by representatives from the Soviet Union, newly independent African states (most notably Ghana and Guinea), Belgium, and the United States, all competing to present their narrative of events. Within the Congo itself, multiple voices—president, prime minister, future coup leader, secessionist leader, local media, citizenry groups, members of the army—articulated either a Congolese national identity or a regional, substate identity. Competing narratives also circulated in international and regional media, pamphlets and fliers passed around at political meetings across the globe, government pronouncements from Western and African capitals, best-selling novels, fictional and documentary films, and the "bush" of the Congolese jungle. Kevin found it necessary to engage in a wide variety of sources when researching, in part to explore the multiplicity and contestedness of discourses, to disaggregate actors, and to explore the complicated ways discourses were circulated and achieved social dominance.

Like Said, Kevin interrogated secondary academic sources as primary examples of discursive construction. Thus, even though the social sciences attempt to maintain a clear distinction between primary and secondary sources, that distinction became blurred. To provide a more contemporary example of how secondary sources can become primary sources within discourses analysis, as we were writing this book, Sunni militants associated with the Islamic State (then known as ISIS) were sweeping across northern Iraq, advancing on Baghdad. On 17 June 2014, BBC News posted an article entitled "Iraq crisis: Media coverage split along sectarian lines," which observed:

> There is a difference too in the language and rhetoric used by the rival TV stations. Al-Iraqiyah TV uses the pejorative name for ISIS "Daish" prefixing the name with "terrorist" when reporting on the Sunni group and other fighters who are joining the armed Islamist

group. On the other side, it refers to Mr Maliki as the "supreme commander of the armed forces".

Al-Rafidayn TV on the other hand uses the words "tribal revolutionaries" to refer to the Sunni fighters and does not mention ISIS in its reports. The channel also uses expressions like "Maliki's army" and "Maliki's militias" to refer to the Iraqi army forces and the phrase "Maliki's war against the people" to refer to the continuing fighting. (BBC 2014)

In this article, we can find a blending of primary and secondary sources that can be utilized for analysis. On one level, the BBC is quoting directly from two TV reports, providing us with rich textual representations to analyze. Indeed, as the BBC implicitly suggests, the different rhetorical practices at play have political implications. The authors recognize contestation over representational practices, which is indeed the focus of discourse analysis. A researcher could push beyond the BBC's journalistic presentation to interrogate the primary texts (Iraqi TV rhetoric) found within the secondary source (the BBC article). But a researcher could also turn the BBC article itself into a primary source and critically interrogate how the BBC report itself is engaged in discursive practices. We believe that such an engagement could possibly result in rich findings, but it also points to an issue that must be addressed by any discourse analyst: when do you stop collecting data?

When Is Enough?

The goal of the analyst is to identify the main structural positions within a discourse by drawing upon the reading of a large number of texts, preferably from a wide variety of sources, media, and genres. But when does one have enough material? In many cases, the researcher may be faced with data overload, a problem Kevin frequently encountered when doing his research for *Imagining the Congo*. For example, when investigating historical representations of the Congo at the time of independence, he was swamped with what often seemed to be relevant data—from *National*

Geographic articles to innumerable political cartoons from the European press to an endless slew of official pronouncements from various governments. If he did not make hard but clear decisions about what counted and what did not (such as limiting review of newspapers and news magazines to a handful), he would probably still be researching today. This underscores our earlier point about delimiting parameters: making a project doable requires making tough decisions, and there needs to be solid intellectual reasons behind those choices. It is important to be as honest and transparent about those decisions as possible.

The ideal situation is that one covers a maximum of eventualities, by reading as much as possible from as many genres as possible. Foucault insisted that one should "read everything, study everything." This is not feasible in practice, and there will therefore always be a risk that some relevant texts are not included. However, almost regardless of the extent of the discourse, relatively few texts will constitute the main points of reference. Therefore at some point one has to be able to decide that one has read enough, even if one has not read everything. Only if a text emerges that cannot be subsumed under one of the main representations that the analysis has already identified must the analysis be adjusted—or perhaps even rewritten entirely.

In her work on discourse analysis, Jennifer Milliken (1999) provides a useful answer when she suggest that an analysis can be said to be complete (or "validated") when, upon adding new texts, one finds that the theoretical categories one has generated also work for those new texts. Milliken writes: "This is also a partial response to the issue of reliability of discourse analyses, i.e., that the interpretation offered has been checked and reworked until it fits with and explains consistently texts that were not originally part of its empirical base" (234–35). Of course, the reliability of any discourse analysis should stand up to external empirical checks. Here, we are making a distinction between empiricism as a *method* (skills of verification, close textual attention, proper sourcing, referencing, and so on) and as a *philosophy of knowledge* (the illusion of delivering fact, truth, and a knowable reality). While we personally reject the latter, we greatly value the former.

SELECTED FURTHER READINGS

Bartelson, Jens. 1995. *A Genealogy of Sovereignty*. Cambridge: Cambridge University Press.

Campbell, David. 1998. *Writing Security: United States Foreign Policy and the Politics of Identity*. Rev. ed. Minneapolis: University of Minnesota Press.

Der Derian, James. 1987. *On Diplomacy: A Genealogy of Western Estrangement*. Oxford: Blackwell.

Hansen, Lene. 2006. *Security as Practice*. London/New York: Routledge.

Klotz, Audie, and Deepa Prakash, eds. 2008. *Qualitative Methods in International Relations*. New York: Palgrave Macmillan.

Mutlu, Can E., and Mark B. Salter, eds. 2013. *Research Methods in Critical Security Studies: An Introduction*. London/New York: Routledge.

Weldes, Jutta. 1999. *Constructing National Interests: The United States and the Cuban Missile Crisis*. Minneapolis: University of Minnesota Press.

5 | Conducting Discourse Analysis

In this chapter we discuss some of the common methodological approaches for conducting discourse analysis in the social sciences. It is worth stressing once again that there is no single way to conduct discourse analysis. We strive to present an overview of the nuts-and-bolts of common approaches. Generally speaking, after conducting the preliminary work discussed in the previous chapter, the discourse analyst submits the "texts" to a close reading (using a variety of possible textual mechanisms) to help delineate the discursive elements at play. This allows the analyst to identify and contextualize specific discourses. As one starts to "unpack" these discourses, a useful strategy is to inventory representations and the asymmetries between them within a given discourse. The analyst can then begin the process of mapping and layering discourses, with an eye on discursive stability, instability, and slippage. Throughout, the analyst should study the ways in which meaning and materiality are related.

In practice, a discourse analyst might employ various textual mechanisms (we explain which of these below) for interpreting a given discourse, before reaching conclusions about the existence and terrain of the discourse. But for heuristic reasons, we feel it best to present a discussion of the destination before engaging in the details of how one might get there. This is akin to familiarizing oneself with a road map before demarcating the specific route to be taken. Therefore, we begin our discussion of the different strategies of conducting discourse analysis in the social sciences by emphasizing what the analyst is ultimately looking for. We then discuss the importance of identifying discourses and locating them in a larger social and historic context. Only after doing so do we then offer an overview of the textual mechanisms for interpreting discourses. We go on to discuss how one inventories representations and maps and layers discourses.

Different Strategies of Conducting Discourse Analysis

Before we get to the micro-level of how one engages specific texts, it is helpful to step back and reflect on what researchers are commonly looking for across the collection of texts they are analyzing. In general, discourse analysts are focusing on either continuity, change, or rupture within discourses. The choice is usually determined by the research questions that are posed. Of course, most research projects are ultimately informed by a bundle of research questions, and one might well combine different strategies of discourse analysis. For example, an examination of how Western societies have historically imagined Russia or the Congo would investigate the continuity and changes within those discourses, as well as when significant ruptures have emerged. But thinking about these three strategies as separate exercises helps illustrate the analytical tactics within each.

Adopting a similar categorization, Can E. Mutlu and Mark B. Salter (2013: 113–14) label these three dominant strategies of discourse analysis *plastic*, *elastic*, and *genealogical*, with each one focusing on continuity, change, or rupture, respectively. They suggest that a plastic approach to discourse analysis focuses on "the identity of linguistic signs and tropes or the persistence of particular metaphorical schema" (114). This approach seeks to uncover an organizing principle within a given discourse, often by using the technique of **intertextuality** (identifying connections of texts and meanings through reference to other texts). As is evident from earlier discussions, Iver's *Uses of the Other* (1999) is an example of this approach.

For Mutlu and Salter, an elastic approach to discourse analysis focuses on the changes and transformations within a discourse over time. This approach seeks to map the emergence or disappearance of signs, tropes, or metaphorical schema and trace any new relations that emerge (2013: 114). As the name implies, this approach is often focused on the malleability of discourses in practice. Kevin's *Imagining the Congo* (2003) sought to investigate these moments of contestation and transformation around the construction of the Congo's identity.

The final category, the genealogical approach to discourse analysis, seeks to investigate the ruptures and breaks within a given discourse, as well as interrogating the silences in order to expose marginalized voices or subjugated knowledges. As Mutlu and Salter write: "The point of the genealogy is not to assume that researchers can discover an origin or ur-text, from which all variants can be understood as deviants, but rather what disappears and what stays and the way these transformations occur with what effect" (2013: 114). Jens Bartelson's examination of sovereignty (1995) is exemplary of the genealogical approach to discourse analysis.

As is always the case, categorization breaks down at some point. While there is value to think in terms of plastic, elastic, and genealogical approaches, these need not be mutually exclusive strategies. One can very well explore both discursive continuity and change within a given research project. The value of making the distinction lies in it allowing researchers to reflect better on what they are seeing at a meta-level when investigating discourses across time and texts: continuity, subtle change, or dramatic breaks.

Identifying Discourses

Because discourse analysis relies heavily on interpretation, one of the first steps must be to identify and locate the discourses under investigation. In her work on Western responses to the Bosnian War, Lene Hansen (2006) offers a very useful presentation of the methodology she employed. Hansen suggests that it is helpful to identify a small number of structuring "basic discourses" that "construct different others with different degrees of radical difference; articulate radically diverging forms of spatial, temporal, and ethical identity; and construct competing links between identity and policy" (52). Hansen identifies a handful of basic discourses within Western policy debates through the reading of multiple texts, but she treats them analytically as ideal-types (that is, stylized representations of what a phenomenon would look like when its internal logic is fully maximized), recognizing but smoothing out differences and degrees. Doing so, according to Hansen, provides "a lens through which a multitude of different representations and policies can be seen as systematically connected" and that allows one to "identify the key points of structuring disagreement within a debate" (2006: 52). For Hansen's approach, there is an important comparative dimension. As she notes, the different "basic discourses" under analysis should advocate different policy options, with at least one in a recognizable position of privilege and the others situating themselves in response to and in criticism of that position (2006: 52–54). For Hansen, this allows the analyst the opportunity to explore how and why one discourse (and the attendant policy proscriptions) became dominant, while recognizing challenges and silences within the debate.

Interpretation requires not just a description of particular representations and representational practices within a discourse but a deeper contextualization within the larger structures of meaning of which they are a part. For Hansen, this entails drawing upon available conceptual histories of the representations chosen: "The importance of conceptual history is not only . . . to create a comparison with past discourses, but also, in Foucault's [1984] terms, to conduct a genealogical reading which traces the constitution of the present concept back in history to understand when and how it was formed as well as how it succeeded in marginalizing other representations" (2006: 53). Kevin has also found Clifford Geertz's "thick description" (1973) a useful concept when locating discourses within a contextualized historical analysis, using the "long conversation" concept of historical anthropologists Jean and John Comaroff (1991) as a way to understand the historic contestation over discourses. In their work on the colonial contact between the Tswana peoples of South Africa and British Christian missionaries, the Comaroffs define the "long conversation" as "the actions and interactions that laid the bases of an intelligible colonial discourse" (1991: 198–99). They argue that there were two faces to this conversation between colonizer and colonized: what was talked *about* and the struggle to gain mastery over the *terms* of the encounter. It may be useful to conceptualize discourses as historically produced within similar "long conversations," where multiple actors contribute and contest the meanings of identities and the terms in which they are expressed. One can recognize how various actors (and the texts they produce) work to establish both what was talked about and the terms of that conversation.

There is a third dimension to the "long conversation" that may be worth highlighting: the struggle over finding and creating an acceptable position or space within the conversation. This refers to the ability to access the "discursive stage" within which to engage in the conversation—as Foucault noted, discourses empower certain people to speak (and act). Delineating and policing this space of discursive legitimacy is an important element in the historical production of discourses, for it underscores again the connections between discourse and power. In Kevin's investigation of the Congo, it was important to note the times, places, and ways in which Congolese actors, as well as other disadvantaged Third World state leaders, were denied access to "legitimate" discursive space. For example, immediately after Congolese independence, Western governments not only intervened directly to deny the seating of Prime Minister Patrice Lumumba's United Nations delegation but also his access to the radio station in his country's capital. Both of these actions effectively limited his ability to articulate and circulate his narratives of Congolese identity within the "long conversation" at the moment of Congolese independence. Thus, silences were actively created within the historic production of a discourse, an interrogation of which can be richly rewarding.

Box 8: Lene Hansen, *Security as Practice: Discourse Analysis and the Bosnian War*

Lene Hansen's *Security as Practice: Discourse Analysis and the Bosnian War* (2006) applied Foucauldian discourse analysis to the study of foreign policy making. At the time, it was already well established that foreign policy could be studied in terms of how agents told stories about themselves and others and what kinds of effects those stories had (Ashley 1989, Campbell 1992, Doty 1996, Weldes 1999). For our purposes, Hansen's book is of major interest for its methodological and methodic rigor in specifying how to study the process of Othering.

Hansen's starting point is that the smallest item of study for the discourse is the statement, the explicit discursive articulation. Hansen's case is how NATO member states related to the 1990s' Bosnian War, and how "the Balkans" came to be represented as violent. We use quotation marks (inverted comas) as a reminder that this representation is just one amongst many ways of articulating the Balkans. Hansen demonstrates how this identification is linked to other concepts used about the Balkans, such as barbarian, underdeveloped, irrational. Since identity is relational, these concepts are held together not only by their being linked as ways of describing the Balkans but also by how these concepts differentiate the Balkans from other identities. Empirically, in the case at hand, the key other identity is Europe, which then becomes the opposite of the Balkans: controlled, civilized, developed, rational.

Foreign policy discourses have historical depth. These depths and the changes that lead from then to now may be charted by looking at historical texts. Hansen suggests that one way of getting at these discursive changes is to study discourses in a tripartite sequence: First, one studies discourse at a certain point A in the past. Then one studies discourse at a later point in time, B, in terms of how the texts published at A were being treated at point B. The third step is to compare how the texts studied were read at point A with how they were read at point B. The comparison identifies the discursive changes. Note how Hansen uses the fact that texts can be tied together not only by being published at the same time (synchronously) but also by being linked by their reception (diachronously). The whole scheme rests on what we call *intertextuality*, that is, how texts are tied together not only by quotation and allusion but also by having been formed according to the same preconditions.

Hansen's research design springs from specification of the four key issues that the researcher has to take a stand on given the framework chosen by the author, namely which selves to study, which texts to locate them in (what she calls intertextual models), which time(s) in which to analyze them (temporal perspective), and which number of events to study. For example, Hansen (2006: 88) chose to study one self, "the West," understood as NATO members states. She chose to study that self in terms of three intertextual models: official discourse, wider policy debates, and academic debates (note that what guarantees a unity between the three is intertextuality itself). A key methodological and empirical point here was how the Western reception in the 1990s of a Carnegie report from 1914 and a travelogue from 1941 turned out to be very important for how the Bosnian War was represented by the West. Hansen's temporal perspective was the 1990s and the number of events studied was one—the Bosnian War.

The book's key empirical findings were that Western discourse went from understanding the event as one where ancient hatreds blossomed and there was little the West could do, to understanding the situation as one where Serbian leaders perpetrated genocide on Bosnians. The effect, that is, the foreign policy choice, of this shift was intervention.

People who are not discourse analysts might well ask why Hansen privileges the choice of selves, and not the event studied. Would it not be truer to the spirit of foreign policy analysis to privilege the event? It would, but since the discourse analysts understands foreign policy in terms of identity, and identity is something pertaining to agents, and not events, the privileging of selves is a logical choice to make.

Textual Mechanisms for Interpreting Discourses

There is no single method for interpreting discourses. As we noted in chapter 3, some analysts might engage specifically in an analysis of theoretical schemata/nodal points or an analysis of prediction/subject-positioning. One might employ a genealogical method, which offers a historical examination that exposes the contingency of contemporary discursive practices. Many analysts employ a **double reading**, or **deconstruction**, method through which the contingent nature of a discourse is revealed by means of a close textual analysis that exposes and troubles the poles of opposition employed within a text to privilege and produce "truths" (Ashley 1988: 235). Methodologically speaking, a text is subjected to a double reading. The first is a descriptive reading in which the analyst identifies and maps the limits of the discursive terrain, the construction of nodal points, and the hierarchical organization around these nodal points. The second is a dialogical reading through which the analyst challenges the supposed fixity and structuring of the text to explore alternative possibilities that the text is implicitly closing off (Shepherd 2008: 28).

All of these methods require a close reading of texts, with an eye for the language being employed. Thus, specific textual mechanisms are important tools for discourse analysis. As Roxanne Doty (1993: 306) has pointed out, "Statements rarely speak for themselves." The reader or listener responds to various mechanisms through which they come to understand meaning. These mechanisms are often deeply naturalized and internalized, so it is often the task of the discourse analyst to denaturalize them and make them visible.

Presupposition and the Creation of Background Knowledges

One textual mechanism is **presupposition**, or the background knowledge that is taken as given. Discourses, through the use of language, construct understandings about the existence of subjects, objects, and the relationships between them. Discourses are potentially at their strongest when those understandings are accepted as given truths, forming a naturalized background knowledge. Statements often presume access to commonly shared structures of knowledge about objects, but their seeming stability should never be assumed. Take the example of "a tree," which might actually mean something different to people living in different cultures or historical eras. A tree might be a natural resource to be preserved, a commodity to be harvested, a living soul force to be honored, or an embodiment of the spirits of the dead to be worshipped. As Doty notes, presupposition "is an important textual mechanism that creates background knowledge and in doing so constructs a particular kind of world in which certain things are recognized as true" (1993: 306). To use an example from Iver's research on Western representations of Russia, the statement "scratch the Russian, and the Tatar will emerge" depends upon (or presupposes) several things: something called a Russian, something called a Tatar, and an intimate relationship between the two. Likewise, JFK's comments about juvenile delinquency presuppose that there are juveniles, delinquency, and a connection between them.

The discourse analyst can examine a given text within a discourse to expose which "natural facts" are being presented, but not called into question. By directing attention to them and potentially calling them into question, the analyst is making visible the work discourses are doing in the production of knowledge, while also opening up space for alternative constructions of knowledge. For instance, what might be gained if we reject an assumed homogenous understanding of "Russian" or "Tatar"? Or, if we trouble seemingly accepted notions of what is understood by "juvenile" or "delinquency"?

Predicate Analysis and the Creation of Subjects

A related textual mechanism is **predication**. Predicate analysis examines the verbs, adverbs, and adjectives that are attached to nouns within specific texts. This approach seeks to expose how certain meanings or capabilities are established, thus enabling actors to understand and act in certain ways. In their work "Soft Bodies, Hard Targets, and Chic Theories," Jennifer Milliken and David Sylvan (1996) use predicate analysis to examine gender and the US bombing in Indochina. By examining archival material, they found that North Vietnam was gendered by US policymakers as masculine, and thus was bombed as a male place (e.g., using high explosives against "hard" targets). South Vietnam, in contrast, was gendered as feminine and thus dealt with as a female place (e.g., using chemical weapons against "soft" targets). In explaining the approach, Milliken writes: "Predications of a noun construct the thing(s) named as a particular sort of thing, with particular features and capacities. Among the objects so constituted may be subjects, defined through being assigned capacities for and modes of acting and interacting" (1999: 232). Predicate analysis thus involves exposing how texts link certain qualities to particular subjects through the use of predicates and the adverbs and adjectives that modify them, such as linking juvenile delinquency to "national" and "problem."

Iver employed predicate analysis in his examination of Western representations of Russia, engaging in close textual readings to systematically illustrate the ways in which certain qualities were connected to the Russian subject. Likewise, Kevin used predicate analysis throughout his work on Western constructions of the Congo. To take but one example, he examined how US discourse on the Congo at the time of its independence involved a construction of the newly elected prime minister, Patrice Lumumba, that overdetermined his eventual removal. He engaged in predicate analysis through a close textual reading of American media coverage and government officials' public statements and internal reports. For example, when he read *Time* magazine's coverage of Lumumba, he found heavy repetition of adjectives such as irrational, erratic, trouble-making, paranoid, unpredictable, reckless, immature, and irresponsible. Evidence of Lumumba's irrationality was found in his nationalist beliefs and criticism of Belgian colonialism.

Thinking about this is terms of methodology, Hansen reminds us that identity construction is not accomplished solely through the designation of one particular sign for the Other or the Self but rather through the location of this sign within a larger system. It is important to consider the processes of linking and differentiation. As Hansen writes, "meaning and identity are constructed through a series of signs that are linked to each other to constitute relations of sameness as well as through a differentiation to another series of juxtaposed signs" (2006: 41–42).

Subject Positioning

In the previous chapter, we discussed the process of **subject positioning** that is at work within a discourse. Part of "doing" discourse analysis can entail making that process explicit. Methodologically, one can uncover the process of subject positioning by interpreting the ways in which text(s) work to create a knowable reality by linking subjects and objects to one another in particular ways. What defines a particular subject is the relative relationships that are constructed between it and other subjects. Oftentimes these relationships are established through the construction of subject positioning based upon opposition or similarity. As Milliken argues, "a text never constructs only one thing," but by constructing (implicitly or explicitly) parallels and contrasts, other things are also constructed (1999: 232).

Taken together, these textual mechanisms involved in subject positioning endow various kinds of subjects with particular attributes and place them in relation with other subjects and objects. Analytically, it is important to recognize that these representations are not neutral or innocuous signifiers, but enable actors to "know" the object and to act upon what they "know." Representations have very real political implications because certain paths of action become possible within distinct discourses, while other paths become unthinkable. Recall the example of the two photos circulated in the media in the aftermath of the August 2005 flooding in New Orleans caused by Hurricane Katrina. The first showed a couple chest-high in water with bags full of groceries. The caption stated that this couple had "found" food in the wake of the flooding. The second photo was of a similar scene, a woman chest-high in water with a bag full of groceries, but she was identified as a "looter." These representations enabled and justified certain actions. Police, for instance, would be expected to assist the couple and to arrest or even shoot the single woman. Thus discursive practices created a truth-effect. As a discourse analyst, one tactic is to expose the practices and possibilities engendered by various textual mechanisms within individual texts and discourses in general. Doing so exposes what Laclau and Mouffe (2001: 112) refer to as *nodal points*, or what Derrida called *master signifiers*. As Laura Shepherd argues, "the nodal points emerge *as* nodal points through the organization and coherence of the text, through predication and subject positioning, but the construction and recognition of nodal points allows 'meaning' and therefore the representational practices that allow their emergence" (2008: 29–30).

Ultimately, the analyst should be attuned to the ways in which differentiation and linking occurs within a discourse. In his examination of the Spanish conquest of the Americas, Tzvetan Todorov (1984) identifies two dominant discourses among the conquistadors. While interrogating a number of diverse texts, Todorov focuses on the discursive constructions produced by Cortés and Las Casas, treating them as "monuments" (in our terminology). Through a close textual reading, Todorov shows the distinct differences in both men's discursive construction of the native "savage."

On the one hand, Cortés constructs native identity as nonhuman, incapable of change, and beyond Christian redemption. Todorov illustrates that within this construction is a discursively produced policy that authorizes violence and annihilation. On the other hand, Las Casas represents the natives as human heathens who could be changed and saved, thus legitimizing a policy of conversion. Lene Hansen points out that the strength of Todorov's discourse analysis was his ability to show not only how these discourses depicted the Other as a "savage" but the different ways in which the term "savage" was linked to other signs within each discourse, resulting in two different identity and policy constructions (2006: 43).

Metaphorical Analysis

Another mechanism for analyzing discourses is **metaphorical analysis**, which entails a critical reading of the metaphors employed and embedded within texts. Metaphors are a textual mechanism used for the transference of meaning, connecting the unfamiliar with the familiar (Rorty 1989: 16). In evoking the familiar through the employment of metaphor, a text works to persuade. In his critical interrogation of the historical narrative (which he likened to an "extended metaphor"), Hayden White argued that metaphors are implicated in the very fabric of social life (1978: 91). If they are to be successful, they must resonate against a set of existing social and cultural representations. The more habitual their use, the more successful they are.

Carol Cohn (1993) uses metaphorical analysis in her interrogation of hegemonic masculinity, militarism, gender, and national security. Using the metaphor of an archeological dig for her methodology, she explores the juxtaposition and layering of many different windows, allowing her to examine the presence of gender as metaphor throughout the national security discourse. As she notes, "Gender discourse is interwoven through national security discourse. It sets fixed boundaries, and in so doing, it skews what is discussed and how it is discussed and how it is thought about" (1993: 242). Employing metaphorical analysis on US Department of Defense official reports, documents, and media accounts, Cohn provides a rich and powerful presentation of how gender permeates national security thinking and practices.

Metaphorical analysis interrogates the ways in which metaphors structure possibilities for human reasoning and action (Milliken 1999: 235). As such, it is related to Roland Barthes's employment of a *semiotic perspective*. Methodologically, the basic task is to identify a series of phenomena referring to each other in a text. These references will be metaphorical, that is, they discuss a phenomenon as if it was another, in terms relating to this other phenomenon. To talk about Mother Sweden, for instance, implies relating the phenomenon nation to the phenomenon family. The point is that one transmits the linguistic luggage associated with "Mother" (origin, care, nurturing, and so forth) to the nation. Barthes's analysis of fashion is instructive: an outfit consists of a set of different pieces of clothing bound together precisely by being a series of different pieces of clothing (e.g., shirt, trousers, shoes, and so on). At the same time, each of these pieces of clothing has an infinite number of combinations (e.g., green short sleeves shirt to striped trousers and brown pointed shoes). But these metaphorical and metonymical series of objects will, when taken together, form a universe from which one must choose a set. By choosing a set of metaphors to talk about a set of phenomena, one re-represents the phenomenon in a particular way. By employing a metaphoric analysis, the discourse analyst seeks to expose the process by which the phenomenon was re-represented, what is engendered, and what alternative re-presentations might be available.

Box 9: Carol Cohn, "Sex and Death in the Rational World of Defense Intellectuals"

In 1987, Carol Cohn published her seminal article "Sex and Death in the Rational World of Defense Intellectuals" in the journal *Signs: Journal of Women in Culture and Society*. Cohn was then associated with the Center for Psychological Studies in the Nuclear Age at the Harvard University Medical School, and her article remains highly influential in women's studies and for a range of feminist analyses across the social sciences, particularly those interested in war, conflict, militarization, and institutions. In the article, Cohn examined the professional discourse used by defense intellectuals, focusing on the sexual and gendered subtext used via metaphors and euphemisms.

Cohn's emphasis was on the role of the specialized discourse of nuclear strategic thinking, what she called the "technostrategic" discourse. As she notes, "I have come to believe that this language both reflects and shapes the nature of the American nuclear strategic project, that it plays a central role in allowing defense intellectuals to think and act as they do, and that feminists who are concerned about nuclear weaponry and nuclear war must give careful attention to the language we choose to use—whom it allows us to communicate with and what it allows us to think as well as say" (1987: 690). Specifically, Cohn was interested in what she referred to as the "ubiquitous weight of gender, both in social relations and in the language itself." As she observed, "it is an almost entirely male world (with the exception of the secretaries), and the language contains many rather arresting metaphors" (1987: 688). Cohn found that the sexualized language (e.g., "deep penetration," "orgasmic whumps," "soft lay downs," and so forth) linked the domesticated and humanized language and imagery in a way that distanced the professionals from the anxieties of war.

What is particularly interesting about Cohn's work is that it combines discourse analysis with participant observation. For her research she spent over a year at the university's center on defense technology and arms control, immersing herself in the lives, lectures, and conversations of defense analysts and professionals. The result is a rich analysis of the professional discourse of Western defense intellectuals, and a useful template for how one can "do" discourse analysis.

Inventorying Representations

A discourse usually contains a dominating representation of reality (*master signifiers* or *nodal points*, to use terms employed earlier) and one or more alternative representations. Discourse analysis therefore is particularly well suited for studying situations where power is maintained by aid of culture and challenged only to a limited degree, that is, what Gramscians call **hegemony**. Structuralists and poststructuralists disagree over whether one can take a small part of the discourse and read it as symptomatic of *all* representations. While structuralists tend to treat limited snapshots of a discourse as illustrative of a larger coherent whole, poststructuralists find the notion of a latent structure simply too deterministic. As poststructuralists ourselves, we think in terms of flow, not control.

Methodologically, the task is to search out and identify these various representations and possible asymmetries between them. We think of this in terms of constructing an *inventory of representations* within a given discourse. But in doing so, one should not enforce strict boundaries between or classifications of representations. The analyst accepts and works with the inherent conflict between and within representations. Monuments frequently position themselves in the discourse by referring (adversarially or sympathetically) to texts that were previously considered monuments. Reading monuments in Russian foreign policy discourse, for example, helped Iver identify adversarial representations (for instance, "Europe is vital, we should learn from it" versus "Europe is rotten, we should isolate ourselves from it"), since these texts, often written at the same time, referred directly to one another. The advantage of a marginal position emerges clearly here for setting up an inventory of representations.

In establishing such an inventory, it is useful to look for repetitions of representations. In Kevin's study of Western representations of the Congo, a number of phrases were repeated with a high degree of regularity, including a portrayal of Africans as primitive, childlike savages and the Congo as a primordial space and, post-Conrad, a proverbial "heart of darkness."[1] Inventorying these representations over time helps contribute to a "map" of the discourses being analyzed, as discussed below. The more such things may be specified empirically, the better the analysis. The ideal is to include as many representations and their variations as possible, and to specify where they are to be found in as high a degree as possible. Demonstrating institutionalized discourse can often simply be done by proving that metaphors regularly appear in the same texts.

Mapping Discourses[2]

Ultimately, a discourse analyst should conduct an investigation of which representations are articulated by a particular discourse or text, how they are linked to achieve discursive stability, where instabilities and slips between these constructions occur, and how competing discourses construct the same representation to different effects (see Hansen 2006: 42). This can be achieved by mapping the discourses under investigation. If inventorying representations is about identifying locations, mapping is about recognizing relations in the constitution of a discourse.

When mapping a discourse, researchers should consider how uncertain or challengeable a given representation may be. Or, to return to the different strategies discussed at the outset, researchers must examine the degree to which representations continue, change, or challenge existing discourses. The limits of discourse are inscribed with varying means and degrees of violence. If there is only one representation, the discourse is closed. This does not mean that it is not politically significant, because it takes a lot of discursive work to maintain a situation where this representation cannot be challenged openly. If attempts to challenge or break with existing discourses are not successful by the text-writer, it is not necessarily because the discourse is successfully policed. On the other end of the spectrum, the field can be said to be open if there are two or more representations and none of them are dominating. Yet it is difficult to imagine a discourse that is entirely open or closed over time. Social relations will always be in flux to some degree.

In addition to analyzing the stability of given representations, it is also important to identify their relative positions within a discourse. There are some inherent challenges to this task, not the least being that the number of permutations of relevant signs is endless, so the range of meanings is in principle infinite. Yet, within political and social life, one can identify contestation between relatively clearly defined positions, which compete to find resonance among a number of carriers. It is desirable to identify these positions when mapping out discourses. Typically, one position will be dominant, and one or two other positions will challenge it on certain points. The dominant position will either present itself as being the way things have "always" been (for instance, a democrat: humans are born free) or hark back to an idealized beginning (a democrat: Athenian democracy broke out of benighted despotism in the middle of the fifth century BCE). Terms mean different things in different epochs, but carriers of a position will tend to tap the advantages of having a long (and presumably dignified) history by acting as if this were not the case (Koselleck 1988).

In mapping discourses, one should show the affinities and differences between representations in order to demonstrate whether they belong to the same discourse. But repetition does not preclude variation or gradual re-presentation, so discourse analysis also seeks to capture the inevitable cultural changes in representations of reality. In his interrogation of Western discourses on the Congo, for example, Kevin's mapping of the "heart of darkness" representation allowed him to recognize that it was being employed during the early 20th century to enable colonization and conquest in the name of spreading civilization and lightness. But by the end of the 20th century, the "heart of darkness" trope was being employed within the discourse to portray the Congo as being beyond hope, suggesting the futility of Western humanitarian intervention and obscuring the cumulative effects of a century of Western intervention and extraction that shaped the conflicts that gripped late 20th-century Central Africa.

In mapping the historical contours of a discourse, it is important that the discourse analyst start with the representations themselves—the stories of how things have "always" been like this or that. For example, Athenian democracy was hardly a democracy by the lights of the 19th century. Neither was the antebellum United States. Arguing that every man is born free and has rights while having a number of living beings around who visibly are not born free and have rights (as slaves, or women, or children) reveals that the discourse has not opened up the possibility that "man" may be someone other than an adult, white male. Within the boundaries of his own political discourse, it was not a problem that George Washington remained a slave owner throughout his adult life.

However, a good discourse analyst should also be able to demonstrate that where the carriers of a position see continuity, there is almost always change. Because of the nature of politics as a structured activity between groups, a discourse is politicized precisely through the evolution of two or a few patterns of meaning, which it is the discourse analyst's task to uncover. It is possible to distinguish between the basic traits of such a meaning pattern (what unites the position) and varieties of it (what differentiates it).

In principle, the discourse will carry with it the "memory" of its own genesis. Showing how each text is made possible by the preceding texts, often it is possible to find a prehistory to the main representation. It is, for example, hard to think of Stalin's funeral oratory for Lenin without having the model of the Russian Orthodox oratory in mind. Methodologically, this is significant because, as a given representation establishes itself in the discourse, one should go back to find "pioneer texts" that foreshadow it. This allows us to make a prediction: if a new main representation of Europe surfaces in Russian discourse during the next years, more likely than not it will be churned out of material that is already present in the discourse.

There are a number of formal and informal practices that determine which representations are allowed into the discourse, and that make it possible for the analyst to map meanings. Among the most obvious are legal systems and censorship, whereby sanctions against violating the boundaries of the discourse are threatened explicitly. For example, in Norwegian nationalist discourse of the 1990s just using the word "race" activated a set of sanctions, foremost among which are laws that prohibit what Americans call "hate speech." The fact that there was no comparable Norwegian concept for the phenomenon of hate speech at that time, and that the American term was used regularly, are data for a discourse analysis of "race."

One can also examine what kind of self-censorship different types of mass media apply and what deviation it takes to provoke more formal sanctions. Legal verdicts on the borderline between incitement to violence and freedom of speech, and the debates surrounding it, would be one of several clues. To study nationalist discourse in the Soviet Union in the 1930s, where every newspaper, radio, and television station sifted what was printed and broadcast, one must start by examining the formal censorship instructions. Thereafter one might look at what unpublished and imported texts circulated, and what incidents resulted in Gulag sentences.

Returning to our previous conversation from chapter 4 about the types of texts utilized by discourse analysis, one should not overlook the usefulness of cultural artifacts with a widespread, so-called popular culture. Discourse analysis is, for example, a rewarding way to examine film, understood as text. Rather than looking at museums, one can look at the reality production that happens in soap operas. If one is to examine the reality of "Germany" in British discourse, then in addition to cases such as bilateral political discourse, EU discourse, and so on, it will also be of interest to look at representations of Germany in magazines, pulp fiction, and imported B movies (where it is still not unusual to find narratives where German Nazis are the crooks), and also on how British tabloids to this day tend to see any foot match between England and Germany as a replay of World War II. It is important for the researcher to be able to point out the interrelation between representations of, say, Germany in popular culture and political discourse about Germany. How does popular culture appear in and relate to political discourse? To what degree do representations from the former result in truth claims in the latter? "Situating" (showing where something can be found, where it is *in situ*, "in place") can be specified as proving intertextuality between expressions, texts, and discourses (see Nexon and Neumann 2006).

Certain analysts are more formal in their mapping than others. We see heuristic value in being stylized. Yet, when discourse analyses are highly formalized, we wonder if the researcher feels the need to present themselves in a certain way within the social sciences in order to get published, or whether it is actually an urge growing out of the text itself, whether it is necessary, and whether it is a market-driven or a scholarly necessity. A degree of self-reflexivity in these matters is always advised.

Layering Discourses

Not all representations within a discourse are equally lasting. They differ in historical depth, in variation, and in degree of dominance/marginalization in the discourse. A final task for the discourse analyst is to demonstrate this. The production of gender is an example. There are a number of biological and social traits that line the boundary between the sexes, from the presence of ovaries to ways of brushing hair away from one's eyes. Few can be counted as unchangeable. However, some are more difficult to alter than others. It is easier to neutralize the gender-specific aspect of the sign "unremunerated domestic labor" than "childbirth."

At this stage, some discourse analysts would cry foul, because they would like to insist that everything is fluid and that nothing should be reified in the analysis. We agree that everything is fluid in principle, but the point here is that not everything is *equally* fluid. Furthermore, it is impossible to analyze something without reifying something else. We have to subsume new phenomena into already existing categories in order to get on with our lives. Arguing that everything is equally fluid makes it impossible to analyze something in its social context and seems to go against what seems to be the very physiological preconditions of our existence as *Homo sapiens*.

Certain representations in a discourse will thus be slower to change than others. Signs that are "good to think" (Lévi-Strauss 1963) and representations of material objects will often be among these. For example, here is a reason why so many languages use the human body to talk about nature, as in the mouth or head of the river or the foot of the mountain. However, material objects can be difficult (though not impossible) to "explain away." But for the study of human behavior, this is not a problem. As Laclau and Mouffe illustrate,

> An earthquake or the falling of a brick is an event that certainly exists, in the sense that it occurs here and now, independently of my will. But whether their specificity as objects is constructed in terms of "natural phenomena" or "expressions of the wrath of God" depends upon the structuring of a discursive field. (2001 [1985]: 108)

As we have asserted throughout, meaning and materiality must be studied together. It is possible to take as one's starting point for a reading of a social event, such as the reasons why JFK declared juvenile delinquency a national problem, that there are a number of recognizable material "facts," including archaeological objects. Any valid representation of the social event must relate to and at the same time study the various representations of the social event without having to hunt some kind of "truth" about it *beyond* accounting for these objects. The question is what the scope or degree of social construction is in the relationship between "fact" and "representation." We should expect greater "inertia" in the representation of material objects than that of other things, but this still does not ensure the place of the objects in the discourse.

This issue also lays bare the metaphors on which the discourse approach rests. Foucault wrote about **archaeology** and **genealogy**, the basic idea being that of things emerging, with some things remaining the same and others changing. An archaeological site will contain certain artifacts that tell of continuity—there will be shards of pottery and traces of funeral rites—and these will vary with the period. But, in a particular site, certain things will remain stable whereas others change. The key, in archaeology as in social analysis, is to specify what changes and what does not, and how. The same is true of genealogy, the basic meaning of which is that you start with one human and trace his or her ancestry. You will tend to find people who become less and less interrelated to one another the further back you go. At some stage, all they have in common is that they are all the ancestor of that particular human.

If some traits unify and some differentiate, it is reasonable to think that the traits that unite are more difficult to change. For example, if one chooses to study German identity, one will find endless variations on which things are thought to be German. If one looks at the question of how the state is related to the nation, the range of meaning will be shorter, perhaps only covering two possibilities: one, that the nation defines the state by being its cultural carrier, *Kulturnation* (cultural nation), or two, that nation and state are both anchored in citizenship, *Verfassungspatriotismus* (constitutional patriotism; see Wæver 1999).

In Iver's doctoral thesis on Russia, he approached this question of layering by postulating explicit and implicit family resemblances across time. The element of Europe as a place to learn from was in evidence at all points in time since the latter half of the 17th century, except for the High Stalinist period (two decades from the early 1930s onward). In later work (Neumann 2004: 21), Iver formalized this step by drawing up a model of Russian discourse on Europe across time, using three layers: basic concepts (state, people, and so on), general policy orientation (isolation, confrontation, learning, and such), and concrete historical examples (pan-Slavism, Bolshevism, early Yeltsin years, among others). At the level of the broad historical sweep, such a mapping of preconditions for action is the end-point of discourse analysis. As should be clear by now from the discussions above, however, there remains endless work of specification on different constitutive relations, close-ups of specific time periods, tailor-making of the analysis to illuminate specific (types of) action, and so forth.

SUGGESTED FURTHER READINGS

Cohn, Carol. 1987. "Sex and Death in the Rational World of Defense Intellectuals," *Signs: Journal of Women in Culture and Society*, 12:4.

Cohn, Carol. 1993. "War, Wimps, and Women: Talking Gender and Thinking War." In Miriam Cooke and Angela Woollacott, eds., *Gendering War Talk*. Princeton: Princeton University Press.

Doty, Roxanne. 1996. *Imperial Encounters*. Minneapolis: University of Minnesota Press.

Silverstein, Michael. 2011. "What Goes Around . . . : Some Schtick from 'Tricky Dick' and the Circulation of U.S. Presidential Image," *Journal of Linguistic Anthropology*, 21:1.

Todorov, Tzvetan. 1984. *The Conquest of America: The Question of the Other*. New York: Harper and Row.

Weber, Cynthia. 1999. *Faking It: U.S. Hegemony in a 'Post-Phallic' Era*. Minneapolis: University of Minnesota Press.

6 | Conclusion

In this concluding chapter, we offer a summation of some of the key points presented throughout the book, and a few final reflections for conducting discourse analysis.

Returning to the opening question of what a discourse is, we offered a definition that established discourse as a system producing a set of statements and practices that, by entering into institutions and appearing like normal, construct the reality of its carriers and maintain a certain degree of regularity in a set of social relations. At its core, we understand discourses to be systems of meaning-production that fix meaning, however temporarily, and enable actors to make sense of the world and to act within it. Attempts to fix the meaning of anything, including the definition of discourse, are always temporary. It would not surprise either of us if readers in the 22nd century find this definition limited or even unrecognizable in their time. Moreover, our understanding of discourse and discourse analysis may differ from those coming from other academic disciplines, such as linguistics. Yet, for our work within the social sciences in this historical moment, we understand discourses as the representational practices through which meanings are generated.

As we have noted, not all social scientists take the same approach to discourses, or to their analysis. Perhaps the most important division is between structuralists and poststructuralists. The difference flows from very different understandings of the philosophy of knowledge. Structuralists, such as Claude Lévi-Strauss, tend to approach social analysis in three steps: (1) look at manifest (observable) structures and fixate them and (2) compare different manifest structures with a view to (3) identify latent structures, understood as the master structure that underlies a society and generates the different manifest structures. Poststructuralists tend to reject the idea that there exists something like a latent structure. Working off of Foucault, they tend to believe that social relations are manifested in language and in those institutions constructed from certain ways of using linguistic categories. Within this understanding of knowledge production, social scientists need not look "behind" language, for all is immediately given in the discourse. Poststructuralists maintain that there is nothing behind, beyond, or outside of discourse. While these differences are extremely important and raise a range of analytic issues, structuralists and poststructuralists share a number of common approaches, methodologically speaking, to how they "do" discourse analysis.

Imagine that you are conducting social research on the concept of juvenile delinquency, to return to the example we have threaded throughout the book. If you narrow down your focus to looking at juvenile delinquency in post–World War II American society (there was something of a "moral panic" about juvenile delinquency in the late 1950s and early 1960s), there is still a wide range of research questions that you could pose, each of which might have a certain methodological approach associated with it. Inspired by Roxanne Doty (1996), we find it useful to generalize between "what," "why," and "how" questions, with discourse analysis primarily related to the last category. Research projects that center around "what" questions are often associated with social research that seeks to create (or "uncover") a linearity of events organized within a historical narrative. For example, discourse analysis would not be an appropriate approach for asking what impact the federal programs established by the Kennedy administration in 1961 had on the levels of juvenile delinquency. Likewise, discourse analysis would be of limited use for the researcher interested in "why" questions, such as why did JFK adopt the policies that he did to deal with the issue of juvenile delinquency. Such questions tend to assume that a certain set of choices and answers preexist, and that a researcher only needs to come upon the right analytical combination to unlock the truth. Both "what" and "why" type research questions are ill-suited for discourse analysis because they either ignore the discursive realm or take it as an unproblematic given. In contrast, discourse analysis is exceptionally well-suited for answering "how" or "how-possible" questions.

So let us assume that you, as a social researcher, are interested in examining how juvenile delinquency became defined in the late 1950s America as a "national problem." As we discussed in chapter 4, it is important to have a degree of cultural competence and historic awareness before embarking on your research. This may involve immersing yourself in secondary literature on American youth culture of the 1950s. As you do so, you should begin to identify the range of texts to analyze. As we discussed, monumental texts should become fairly easy to identify, but there are no standard measures by which to choose all of the texts for your research project. We maintain that the criteria you employ should be clearly justified, not just to yourself but to your potential readers as well. This same applies to the criteria you use to delimit the scope of your project and your discursive "data set."

As you move forward, one question you can ask yourself is whether you are interested in focusing on continuity, change, or rupture within the discourse of juvenile delinquency, or some combination of the three. As we noted, these need not be mutually exclusive strategies for the researcher, but there is value in being reflexive about the distinction—and your preferences—at the meta-level as you begin your investigation of the discourse(s) across time and texts. A focus on continuity requires a focus on uncovering an organizing principle within a given discourse, while a focus on change is more concerned with tracking the emergence or disappearance of signs, tropes, or metaphorical schema. Examining the ruptures and breaks within a given discourse also uncovers marginalized voices or subjugated knowledges, in this case possibly the voices of dispossessed youth and other underrepresented sectors of American society.

Having identified the texts to be examined, you could then submit those texts—be they government reports and policies, scholarly and media treatises on the "scourge" of juvenile delinquency, or popular texts and movies such as *Blackboard Jungle* or *Rebel Without a Cause*—to a close textual reading. In doing so, you would begin to see how seemingly "natural" facts about juvenile delinquency—be they general background knowledge, common sense understanding of the youth and youth culture, or accepted wisdom on the relationships between subjects (such as race and crime)—are constructed within these discourses. You could adopt a variety of methods of analysis. For instance, you could explore the contingent nature of the 1950s discourse on juvenile delinquency by exposing and troubling the poles of opposition within a text that produce seeming "truths" (such as the core normal/abnormal opposition underpinning much of the discourses on youth culture in general). You could also adopt a juxtaposition method that compares the dominant discourse with alternative interpretations around specific issues or events, such as the near-riot at the first rock and roll concert, which was held on March 21, 1952, in Cleveland. You could also adopt a genealogical or archeological method to expose the contentious contingency of contemporary discursive practices, perhaps around the concept of "teenager" that emerged in the 1950s.

Regardless of the specific method or methods employed, an analyst should work to identify and inventory the representational practices that constitute the discourses at work. For example, you could identify and inventory the representational practices employed in the 1950s that are working to construct and fix the meaning of juvenile delinquency. In doing so, you can begin to map these discourses, showing affinities and differences between representations in order to demonstrate whether they belong to the same discourse, with an eye for variation, re-presentation, and emerging changes in representations of juvenile delinquency. You could also work to layer the discourses at play, noting how representations differ in historical depth, in variation, and in degree of dominance/marginalization in the discourse. Throughout the 1950s, for example, the meaning of juvenile delinquency was highly contingent with competing attempts to define and fix its meaning. Mapping and layering discourses would allow you to examine attempts to link the concept to other discourses of race, education, parenting, masculinity, hetero-normativity, patriotism and citizenship, drugs and alcohol, miscegenation, and music, to name but a few. Examining the ways in which juvenile delinquency was discursively linked to, say, anxieties about effeminate fathers, poor schools, or the "primitive" beats of rock 'n' roll, opens up fertile ground to explore how these discourses were intimately tied to power and had significant material implications for the production and regulation of the social world.[1]

While conducting your research, you should be attuned to both the presence and absence of conflict over fixing meanings. When examining the texts operating within a given historic moment, such as in 1950s

America, the presence of conflict usually means something new is emerging, something that is meeting various attempts at contestation from those who dominate the discourse (such as educators or scholars on youth culture). But as we warned in chapter 4, searching for the presence of commotion can be a methodological problem, since realities are maintained by the frequent repetition and confirmation of representations. The absence of conflict does not mean that the discourse in question is fixed and not contested. You have to use more time and mental energy to work out how and why things remain unaltered. If one fails to detect these processes of power, then the analysis easily becomes a shallow description of the boundaries of the discourse and its domination.

Of course, the discourse analyst is an active agent in the production of discourses herself. As poststructuralists, we are aware of the ironic position that, just as discourses do not reveal any great meta-"truth," neither does an analysis of discourses. There is simply no way to step outside of interpretation. There is no objective Truth to discover, only competing interpretations to navigate. This leads us to offer a few final observations that we hope may be of use to the social researcher embarking on discourse analysis. While we do not believe that there is a *terra firma* upon which objectivity rests, we do believe there are a few simple rules to "good" analysis.

First of all, one must always ensure that there is enough supporting evidence to back up any interpretation. As a researcher, it will often seem obvious that the bulk of our data is pointing to a certain set of interpretations. But as writers, we need to convey that information to our readers. This may seem intuitive, but it is worth noting how often researchers fail to convey the depth and breadth of their evidence in their writings, resulting in readers questioning their claims for seemingly being highly speculative. Likewise, the validity of one's interpretation is often measured by its logical coherence. Always ask yourself these questions: Do your interpretations make sense to you and your readers? Do they provide a reasonable answer for the questions you were trying to answer? Are they more convincing than alternative interpretations? If not, then you need to try again.

Above all else, you must pay attention to the choices you have made throughout your research—from the forming of the research question, to the delineation of texts under analysis, to how you chose to write up your findings—and be reflexive about those decisions and why you've made them (see Neumann and Neumann 2015). As Mutlu and Salter (2013: 118) have pointed out "language is both social and political." As a discourse analyst, you both study language and convey your findings through language. This requires all of us to be self-reflective about our role as social researchers. Ultimately, you should strive for transparency and clarity in order to avoid misinterpretations and misunderstandings. This applies to all social researchers, whether they are employing discourse analysis or not.

Notes

1. Due to the space restrictions, this book focuses on conducting discourse analysis on written and spoken texts. For conducting discourse analysis on visual imagery, see Rose 2013, Hansen 2011, and Mutlu and Salter 2013.

CHAPTER 2

1. Later, when he reflects on the difference between archaeology and genealogy, he comments on the relationship between them: "If we were to characterize it in two terms, 'archaeology' would be the appropriate methodology of this analysis of local discursivities, and 'genealogy' would be the tactics whereby, on the basis of the descriptions of these local discursivities, the subjected knowledges which were thus released would be brought into play" (Foucault 1980: 85).

2. Common, but not unchallenged: "Discourse analysis focuses on the structure of naturally occurring spoken language, as found in such 'discourses' as conversations, interviews, commentaries, and speeches. Text analysis focuses on the structure of written language, as found in such 'texts' as essays, notices, road signs, and chapters. But this distinction is not clear-cut, and there have been many other uses of these labels. In particular, 'discourse' and 'text' can be used in a much broader sense to include all language units with a definable communicative function, whether spoken or written. Some scholars talk about 'spoken or written discourse'; others about 'spoken or written texts'" (Crystal 1987: 116).

CHAPTER 3

1. De Beauvoir, obviously, wrote before the concept discourse analysis was established and before Althusser introduced the concept interpellation (in 1970).

2. Milliken has cited Bruce Lincoln's (1989) work on cultural myths as an exemplar of conducting such research: "Lincoln shows how myths as cultural resources have been articulated in different ways by subgroups in societies so as to produce the conditions for resistance and, indeed, for social change" (Milliken 1999: 245)

3. This section borrows liberally from Iver's (Neumann 2002a) "Returning Practice to the Linguistic Turn: The Case of Diplomacy," *Millennium* 32 (3): 627–52.

4. For a slightly different approach—specifically one from linguistic anthropology—see the works of Michael Silverstein (esp., 1998 and 2004). Though often quite dense, his work on culture and discourse has been influential for many researchers. His writings on the political "message" are particularly engaging and potentially rewarding methodologically (see 2011a, 2011b).

5. Foucault's celebrated solicitation, "We need to cut off the King's head, in political theory that has still to be done" (Foucault 1980: 121), is thus still pressingly relevant. Note that the intention is not to wave analyses of formal organization farewell: "I don't want to say that the State isn't important; what I want to say is that relations of power [. . .] necessarily extend beyond the limits of the State" (Foucault 1979: 38).

CHAPTER 4

1. "sXe" refers to the "straightedge" movement within punk that, among other things, rejects drug and alcohol use. "Queercore" is a movement that foregrounds LGBTQ issues within punk communities and society in general.

CHAPTER 5

1. Ironically, few people who drew on Conrad's metaphor seemed to grasp that the heart of darkness in his eponymous story was London, not the Congolese jungle.

2. This section borrows elements from Iver Neumann (2008), "Discourse Analysis," in Audie Klotz and Deepa Prakash, eds., *Qualitative Methods in International Relations* (Houndmills, UK: Palgrave Macmillan).

CHAPTER 6

1. Ultimately, as analysts of discourses, we reject notions that knowledge is separate from the social realm. We regard knowledge as constitutive of reality. The material world does not present itself as self-evident to its inhabitants. Rather, societies construct and attach meanings and values to the material world around us. They do so through the construction of discourses. As social researchers, we can critically engage and evaluate the discourses that constitute our social reality, from the category of "teenager" to the concept of "juvenile delinquency."

Bibliography

Althusser, Louis. 1970. "Idéologie et appareills ideologiques d'État (Notes pour une recherché) [Ideology and Ideological State Apparatuses]." *La Pensée*. 151.

Andersen, Niels Akerstrom. 2003. *Discursive Analytical Strategies: Understanding Foucault, Koselleck, Laclau, Luhmann*. Bristol: Policy Press.

Ashley, Richard. 1988. "Untying the Sovereign State: A Double Reading of the Anarchy Problematique." *Millennium* 17 (2): 227–62.

Ashley, Richard. 1989. "Living on Border Lines: Man, Poststructuralism and War." In James Der Derian and Michael Shapiro, eds., *International/Intertextual Relations*, 259–323. Lexington: Lexington Books.

Bakhtin, Mikhail M. 1981. *The Dialogic Imagination: Four Essays*. Austin: University of Texas Press.

Bakhtin, Mikhail M. 1986. *Speech Genres and Other Late Essays*. Austin: University of Texas Press.

Bakhtin, Mikhail M. [1963] 1993. *Problems of Dostoevsky's Poetics*. Minneapolis: University of Minnesota Press.

Ball, Terence. 1988. *Transforming Political Discourse: Political Theory and Critical Conceptual History*. Oxford: Blackwell.

Banta, Benjamin. 2013. "Analysing Discourse as a Causal Mechanism." *European Journal of International Relations* 19 (2): 379–402.

Barnes, Barry. 2001. "Practice as Collective Action." In Theodore R. Schatzky, Karin Knorr Cetina, and Eike von Savigny, eds., *The Practice Turn in Contemporary Theory*, 17–28. London: Routledge.

Barnes, Trevor J., and James Duncan. 1992. "Introduction." In Barnes and Duncan, eds., *Writing Worlds: Discourse, Text and Metaphor in the Representation of Landscape*, 1–17. London and New York: Routledge.

Bartelson, Jens. 1995. *A Genealogy of Sovereignty*. Cambridge: Cambridge University Press.

Bartelson, Jens. 2014. *Sovereignty as Symbolic Form*. New York: Routledge. Kindle Edition.

Barth, Fredrik. 1993. *Balinese Worlds*. Chicago: University of Chicago Press.

Barthes, Roland. 1977 [1968]. "The Death of the Author." In *Image Music Text*, 142–48. London: Fontana.

Barthes, Roland. 1981. "The Discourse of History." *Comparative Criticism* 3:3–20.

BBC. 2014. "Iraq Crisis: Media Coverage Split Along Sectarian Lines." June 17. http://www.bbc.com/news/world-middle-east-27884167 (accessed June 18, 2014).

Bedau, M.A., and P. Humphreys, eds. 2008. *Emergence: Contemporary Readings in Philosophy and Science*. Cambridge: MIT Press.

Bøås, Morten, and Kevin Dunn. 2013. *Politics of Origin in Africa: Autochthony, Citizenship and Conflict*. London: Zed Press.

Bourdieu, Pierre. 1977. *Outline of a Theory of Practice*. Cambridge: Cambridge University Press.

Bourdieu, Pierre. 1991. *Language and Symbolic Power*. Cambridge: Polity.

Brown, Callum G. 2005. *Postmodernism for Historians*. London: Pearson Longman.

Butler, Judith. 1993. *Bodies That Matter: On the Discursive Limits of 'Sex.'* London: Routledge.

Campbell, David. 1998. *Writing Security: United States Foreign Policy and the Politics of Identity*, rev. ed. Minneapolis: University of Minnesota Press.

Campbell, David. 1993. *Politics Without Principles: Sovereignty, Ethics, and the Narratives of the Gulf War*. Boulder: Lynne Rienner.

Casey, Caroline. 1995. *Work, Self and Society: After Industrialism*. London: Routledge.

Chouliaraki, Lilie, and Norman Fairclough. 1999. *Discourse in Late Modernity: Rethinking Critical Discourse Analysis*. Edinburgh: Edinburgh University Press.

Cohen, L., L. Manion, and K. Morrison. 2008. *Research Methods in Education*, 6th ed. London: Routledge Falmer.

Cohn, Carol. 1987. "Sex and Death in the Rational World of Defense Intellectuals." *Signs: Journal of Women in Culture and Society* 12 (4): 687–718.

Cohn, Carol. 1993. "War, Wimps, and Women: Talking Gender and Thinking War." In Miriam Cooke and Angela Woollacott, eds., *Gendering War Talk*. Princeton: Princeton University Press.

Comaroff, Jean, and John Comaroff. 1991. *Of Revelation and Revolution: Christianity, Colonialism, and Consciousness in South Africa,* Vol. I. Chicago and London: University of Chicago Press.

Connolly, William. 1991. *Identity\Difference: Democratic Negotiations of Political Paradox*. Ithaca: Cornell University Press.

Coyle, A. 1995. "Discourse Analysis." In G. Breakwell, S. Hammond, and C. Fife-Schaw, eds., *Research Methods in Psychology*, 243–58. London: Sage.

Crystal, David. 1987. *The Cambridge Encyclopedia of Language*. Cambridge: Cambridge University Press.

de Beauvoir, Simone. 2011 [1949]. *The Second Sex*. New York: Vintage.

de Certeau, Michel. 1984. *The Practice of Everyday Life*. Berkeley: University of California Press.

de Saussure, Ferdinand. 1986 [1916]. *Course in General Linguistics*. Ed. C. Bally and A. Sechehaye. La Salle: Open Court.

Dean, Mitchell. 1994. *Critical and Effective Histories. Foucault's Methods and Historical Sociology*. London: Routledge.

Der Derian, James. 1987. *On Diplomacy: A Genealogy of Western Estrangement*. Oxford: Blackwell.

Derrida, Jacques. 1974. *Of Grammatology*. Baltimore: John Hopkins University Press.

Derrida, Jacques. [1967] 1978. *Writing and Difference*. London: Routledge & Kegan Paul.

Derrida, Jacques. 1981. *Positions*. Chicago: University of Chicago Press.

Doty, Roxanne. 1993. "Foreign Policy as Social Construction: A Post-Positivist Analysis of U.S. Counterinsurgency Policy in the Philippines." *International Studies Quarterly* 37:297–320.

Doty, Roxanne Lynn. 1996. *Imperial Encounters*. Minneapolis: University of Minnesota Press.

Dreyfus, Hubert, and Paul Rabinow. 1984. *Michel Foucault: Beyond Structuralism and Hermeneutics*. Chicago: University of Chicago Press.

du Gay, Paul. 1996. *Consumption and Identity at Work*. London: Sage.

Dunn, Kevin C. 2003. *Imagining the Congo*. New York: Palgrave Macmillan.

Dunn, Kevin. 2004. "Fear of a Black Planet: Anarchy Anxieties and Post-Colonial Travel." *Third World Quarterly* 25 (3): 483–99.

Dunn, Kevin. 2009. "Contested State Spaces: African National Parks and the State." *European Journal of International Relations* 15 (3): 423–46.

Dunn, Kevin. 2012. "Anarcho-Punk and Resistance in Everyday Life." *Journal of Punk and Post-Punk Studies* 1 (2): 201–18.

Dunn, Kevin. Forthcoming. *Global Punk: Resistance and Rebellion in Everyday Life*. New York: Bloomsbury Academic.

Durkheim, Emile. 1982 [1895]. *The Rules of Sociological Method*. New York: Simon and Schuster.

Elias, Norbert, and Eric Dunning. 1986. *Quest for Excitement: Sport and Leisure in the Civilizing Process*. Blackwell: Oxford.

Fairclough, Norman. 1992. *Discourse and Social Change*. Cambridge: Polity Press.

Fairclough, Norman. 1995. *Critical Discourse Analysis: The Critical Study of Language*. London: Longman.

Fairclough, Norman. 2003. *Analysing Discourse*. London: Routledge.

Finstad, Liv. 2000. *Politiblikket* [The Police Gaze]. Oslo: Pax.

Foucault, Michel. 1970 [1969]. *Archaeology of Knowledge*. London: Tavistock.

Foucault, Michel. 1973. *The Order of Things*. New York: Pantheon.

Foucault, Michel. 1977 [1975]. *Discipline and Punish: The Birth of the Prison*. New York: Vintage Books.

Foucault, Michel. 1978. *The History of Sexuality, Vol. 1: An Introduction*. Harmondsworth: Penguin.

Foucault, Michel. 1979. *Discipline and Punish. The Birth of the Prison*. New York: Vintage.

Foucault, Michel. 1980. "Two Lectures." In *Power/Knowledge: Selected Interviews and Other Writings 1972–1977*, ed. Colin Gordon. Brighton: Harvester.

Foucault, Michel. 1981. "The Order of Discourse." In R. Young, ed., *Untying the Text: A Post-structuralist Reader*, 48–78. London: Routledge & Kegan Paul.

Foucault, Michel. 1984. "Space, Knowledge, and Power. Foucault Interviewed by Paul Rabinow." In *The Foucault Reader*, ed. Paul Rabinow, 239–56. New York: Pantheon.

Foucault, Michel. 1985. *The Uses of Pleasure. The History of Sexuality, Vol. 2*. Harmondsworth: Penguin.

Foucault, Michel. 2000 [1978]. "Governmentality." In *Power: The Essential Works of Foucault, 1954–1984*, ed. J. D. Faubion, 2001–2022. London: Penguin.

Frykman, Jonas, and Ingvar Løfgren. 2003. *Culture Builders: A Historical Anthropology of Middle Class Life*. New Brunswick: Rutgers University Press.

Fukuyama, Francis. 1989. "The End of History." *National Interest* 16 (Summer): 3–18.

Gee, James Paul. 1996. *Sociolinguistics and Literacies: Ideology in Discourses*, 2nd ed. London: Taylor & Francis.

Gee, James Paul. 1999. *An Introduction to Discourse Analysis: Theory and Method*. New York: Routledge.

Gee, James Paul. 2005. *An Introduction to Discourse Analysis: Theory and Method*, 2nd ed. New York: Routledge.

Gee, James Paul. 2011. *How to Do Discourse Analysis: A Toolkit*. New York: Routledge.

Geertz, Clifford. 1973. *The Interpretation of Culture*. New York: Basic Books.

Gutting, Gary. 1994. "Introduction. Michel Foucault: A User's Manual." In Gary Gutting, ed., *The Cambridge Companion to Foucault*, 1–27. Cambridge: Cambridge University Press.

Habermas, Jürgen. 1987. *The Philosophical Discourse of Modernity: Twelve Lectures*. Cambridge: Polity.

Hansen, Lene. 2006. *Security as Practice: Discourse Analysis and the Bosnian War*. London: Routledge.

Hansen, Lene. 2011. "Theorizing the Image for Security Studies: Visual Securitization and the Muhammad Cartoon Crisis." *European Journal of International Relations* 17 (1): 51–74.

Howarth, David, and Yannis Stavrakakis. 2000. "Introducing Discourse Theory and Political Analysis." In D. Howarth and A. Norval, eds., *Discourse Theory and Political Analysis*, 1–23. Manchester: Manchester University Press.

Huysmans, Jef. 2006. *The Politics of Insecurity: Fear, Migration and Asylum in the EU*. London and New York: Routledge.

Jackson, Patrick T. 2011. *The Conduct of Inquiry in International Relations: Philosophy of Science and Its Implications for the Study of World Politics*. London and New York: Routledge.

Jackson, Richard. 2005. *Writing the War on Terrorism*. Manchester: Manchester University Press.

Kaplan, Robert. 1994. "The Coming Anarchy." *Atlantic Monthly*. February.

Kennedy, John F. 1961. "Remarks Upon Signing the Juvenile Delinquency and Youth Offenses Control Act." September 22. Online at http://www.presidency.ucsb.edu/ws/?pid=8347 (accessed October 2, 2014).

Keohane, Robert. 1998. "Beyond Dichotomy: Conversations between International Relations and Feminist Theory." *International Studies Quarterly* 42 (1): 193–97.

Kiersey, Nicholas J., and Iver B. Neumann, eds. 2013. *Battlestar Galactica and International Relations: Popular Culture and World Politics*. London: Routledge.

Klotz, Audie, and Deepa Prakash, eds. 2008. *Qualitative Methods in International Relations*. New York: Palgrave Macmillan.

Koselleck, Reinhart. 1988. *Critique and Crises*. Cambridge: MIT Press.

Kress, Gunther, and Theo van Leeuwen. 1996. *Reading Images: The Grammar of Visual Design*. Victoria: Deakin University Press.

Kuhn, Thomas. 1970. *The Structure of Scientific Revolutions*. Chicago: University of Chicago Press.

Kurki, Milja. 2008. *Causation in International Relations: Reclaiming Causal Analysis*. Cambridge: Cambridge University Press.

Laclau, Ernesto. 1996. *Emancipation(s)*. London: Verso.

Laclau, Ernesto, and Chantal Mouffe. 2001 [1985]. *Hegemony and Socialist Strategy: Towards a Radical Democratic Politics*. London: Verso.

Latour, Bruno, and Steve Woolgar. 1986. *Laboratory Life: The Construction of Scientific Facts*. Princeton: Princeton University Press.

Lévi-Strauss, Claude. 1963. *Structural Anthropology*. New York: Basic.

Lobo-Guerrero, Luis. 2013. *Insuring War: Sovereignty, Security and Risk*. London: Routledge.

Lukes, Steven. 1974. *Power: A Radical View*. London: Macmillan.

Mbembe, Achille. 1992. "Provisional Notes on the Postcolony." *Africa* 62 (1): 3–37.

Mbembe, Achille. 2001. *On the Postcolony.* Berkeley: University of California Press.

Mearsheimer, John. 1994/1995. "The False Promise of International Institutions." *International Security* 19 (3): 5–49.

Miller, A. 2010. "Realism." In E. N. Zalta, ed., *The Stanford Encyclopedia of Philosophy.* Online at http://plato.stanford.edu/archives/sum2010/entries/realism.

Milliken, Jennifer. 1999. "The Study of Discourse in International Relations. A Critique of Research and Methods." *European Journal of International Relations* 5 (2): 225–54.

Milliken, Jennifer, and D. Sylvan. 1996. "Soft Bodies, Hard Targets, and Chic Theories: US Bombing Policy in Indochina." *Millennium* 25 (2): 321–59.

Mills, Sue. 1997. *Discourse.* London: Routledge.

Mutlu, Can E., and Mark B. Salter, eds. 2013. *Research Methods in Critical Security Studies: An Introduction.* London and New York: Routledge.

Neumann, Cecilie Basberg, and Iver B. Neumann. 2015. "Uses of the Self: Two Ways of Thinking about Scholarly Situatedness and Method." *Millennium* 45 (3): 798–819.

Neumann, Iver B. 1996. *Russia and the Idea of Europe: A Study in Identity and International Relatons.* London: Routledge.

Neumann, Iver B. 1999. *Uses of the Other: "The East" in European Identity Formation.* Minneapolis: University of Minnesota Press.

Neumann, Iver B. 2001. *Norge—en kritikk. Begrepsmakt i Europa-debatten.* Oslo: Pax.

Neumann, Iver B. 2002a. "Returning Practice to the Linguistic Turn: The Case of Diplomacy." *Millennium* 32 (3): 627–52.

Neumann, Iver B. 2002b. "This Little Piggy Stayed at Home: Why Norway Is Not a Member of the EU." In Lene Hansen and Ole Wæver, eds., *European Integration and National Identity: The Challenge of the Nordic States.* London: Routledge.

Neumann, Iver B. 2008. "Discourse Analysis." In Audie Klotz and Deepa Prakash, eds., *Qualitative Methods in International Relations.* New York: Palgrave.

Neumann, Iver B. 2012. *At Home with the Diplomats: Inside a European Foreign Ministry*. Ithaca: Cornell University Press.

Newbury, David. 1998. "Understanding Genocide." *African Studies Review* 41 (1): 73–98.

Nexon, Daniel, and Iver B. Neumann. 2006. *Harry Potter and International Relations*. Lanham, MD: Rowman & Littlefield.

Nietzsche, Friedrich. 1967 [1887]. *On the Genealogy of Morals*. New York: Vintage.

Nietzsche, Friedrich. 1967. *Will to Power*. New York: Vintage.

Pring, R. 2000. *Philosophy of Educational Research*. London: Continuum.

Rapley, T. 2008. *Doing Conversation, Discourse, and Document Analysis*. London: Sage.

Ringmar, Erik. 1996. *Identity, Interest and Action: A Cultural Explanation of Sweden's Intervention in the Thirty Years War*. Cambridge: Cambridge University Press.

Rorty, Richard. 1989. *Contingency, Irony, and Solidarity*. Cambridge: Cambridge University Press.

Rose, Gillian. 2013. *Visual Methodologies: An Introduction to Researching with Visual Materials*, 3rd ed. London: Sage.

Said, Edward. 1978. *Orientalism*. Harmondsworth: Penguin.

Schatzki, Theodore R. 2001. "Practice Mind-ed Orders." In Theodore R. Schatzky, Karin Knorr Cetina, and Eike von Savigny, eds., *The Practice Turn in Contemporary Theory*, 42–55. London: Routledge.

Scott, James C. 1985. *Weapons of the Weak: Everyday Forms of Peasant Resistance*. New Haven: Yale University Press.

Scott, James C. 1998. *Seeing Like a State: How Certain Schemes to Improve the Human Condition Have Failed*. New Haven: Yale University Press.

Shapiro, Michael J. 1981. *Language and Political Understanding: The Politics of Discursive Practices*. New Haven: Yale University Press.

Shapiro, Michael J., ed. 1984. *Language and Politics*. New York: New York University Press.

Shapiro, Michael J. 1988. *The Politics of Representation: Writing Practices in Biography, Photography, and Policy Analysis*. Madison: University of Wisconsin Press.

Shepherd, Laura. 2008. *Gender, Violence and Security*. London: Zed Books.

Silverstein, Michael. 1998. "The Improvisational Performance of Culture in Realtime Discursive Practice." In R. Keith Sawyer, ed., *Creativity in Performance*, 265–312. Greenwich: Ablex.

Silverstein, Michael. 2004. "'Cultural' Concepts and the Language-Culture Nexus." *Current Anthropology* 45 (5): 621–52.

Silverstein, Michael. 2011a. "The 'Message' in the (Political) Battle." *Language & Communication* 31:203–16.

Silverstein, Michael. 2011b. "What Goes Around . . . : Some Schtick from 'Tricky Dick' and the Circulation of U.S. Presidential Image." *Journal of Linguistic Anthropology* 21 (1): 54–77.

Somers, Margaret R. 1994. "The Narrative Constitution of Identity: A Relational and Network Approach." *Theory and Society* 23 (5): 605–49.

Spivak, Gayatri Chakravorty. 1987. *In Other Worlds: Essays in Cultural Politics*. New York: Methuen.

Sunderland, J. 2004. *Gendered Discourses*. London: Palgrave.

Swidler, Ann. 2001. "What Anchors Cultural Practices." In Theodore R. Schatzki, Karin Knorr Cetina, and Eike von Savigny, eds., *The Practice Turn in Contemporary Theory*, 74–92. London: Routledge.

Taylor, Stephanie. 2001. "Locating and Conducting Discourse Analytic Research." In Margaret Wetherell, Stephanie Taylor, and Simeon Yates, eds., *Discourse as Data: A Guide for Analysis*, 5–48. London: Sage.

Titscher, Stefan, Michael Meyer, Ruth Wodak, and Eva Vetter. 2000. *Methods of Text and Discourse Analysis*. London: Sage.

Todorov, Tzvetan. 1984. *The Conquest of America: The Question of the Other*. New York: Harper and Row.

Torfing, Jacob. 1999. *New Theories of Discourse: Laclau, Mouffe and Zizek*. Oxford: Blackwell Press.

Torfing, Jacob. 2005. *Discourse Theory in European Politics*. Basingstoke: Palgrave Macmillan.

van Dijk, T. 2001. "Critical Discourse Analysis." In D. Tannen, D. Schiffrin, and H. Hamilton, eds., *Handbook of Discourse Analysis*, 352–71. Oxford: Blackwell.

van Leeuwen, Theo. 2008. *Discourse and Practice: New Tools for Critical Discourse Analysis*. Oxford: Oxford University Press.

Wæver, Ole. 2002. "Identity, Community and Foreign Policy: Discourse

Analysis as Foreign Policy Theory." In Lene Hansen and Ole Wæver, eds., *European Integration and National Identity: The Challenge of the Nordic States*, 1–23. London: Routledge.

Walt, Stephen. 1991. "The Renaissance of Security Studies." *International Studies Quarterly* 35 (2): 211–39.

Weber, Cynthia. 1995. *Simulating Sovereignty*. Cambridge: Cambridge University Press.

Weber, Cynthia. 1999. *Faking It: U.S. Hegemony in a 'Post-Phallic' Era*. Minneapolis: University of Minnesota Press.

Weldes, Jutta. 1999. *Constructing National Interests: The United States and the Cuban Missile Crisis*. Minneapolis: University of Minnesota Press.

Weldes, Jutta, and D. Saco. 1996. "Making State Action Possible: The United States and the Discursive Construction of 'The Cuban Problem,' 1960–1994." *Millennium: Journal of International Studies* 25 (2): 361–95.

Wetherell, Margaret, Stephanie Taylor, and Simeon Yates, eds. 2001. *Discourse as Data: A Guide for Analysis*. London: Sage.

White, Hayden. 1978. *Tropics of Discourse: Essays in Cultural Criticism*. Baltimore: Johns Hopkins University Press.

Wiggerhaus, Rolf. 1994. *The Frankfurt School: Its History, Theories and Political Significance*. Cambridge: MIT Press.

Williams, Patrick, and Laura Chrisman, eds. 1993. *Colonial Desire: Hybridity, Theory, Culture and Race*. London: Routledge.

Willis, Paul E. 1977. *Learning to Labour: How Working Class Kids Get Working Class Jobs*. Farnborough: Saxon House.

Wittgenstein, Ludwig. 1958 [1953]. *Philosophical Investigations*. Oxford: Blackwell.

Wolff, Larry. 1994. *Inventing Eastern Europe: The Map of Civilization on the Mind of the Enlightenment*. Stanford: Stanford University Press.

Yanow, Dvora. 1996. *How Does a Policy Mean? Interpreting Policy and Organizational Actions*. Washington, DC: Georgetown University Press.

Žižek, Slavoj. 1990. "Beyond Discourse Analysis." In Ernesto Laclau, ed., *New Reflections on the Revolution of Our Time*, 249–60. London: Verso.

Index

action: Bruno Latour and, 77; discourse
  and, 8, 60–61, 63, 66; Michel Foucault
  and, 68; pattern of, 69; preconditions
  for, 68; subjects and, 76
action-taking, 45
adaptation, 79
agency, 35–36, 58
Althusser, Louis, 132n1
Annales d'histoire économique et sociale,
  27
Annales School, 27
anthropology, 69, 85, 132n4
archaeology, 21, 23, 29, 114, 123, 131n1
The Archaeology of Knowledge (Foucault),
  9, 20–23, 21–23, 26
archive, 68–69
archives, 12
articulation, 50
artifacts, 120
assumptions, 59–60
authority, 59–60

background knowledge, 110–11
Bakhtin, Mikhail, 25, 27, 96
Ball, Terence, 57
Banta, Benjamin, 38
Barnes, Trevor, 54
Barth, Fredrick, 20
Barthes, Roland, 46, 115
Bartleson, Jens, 3–4, 18, 70–73, 105
base, 79
Bedau, M. A., 37
Birmingham School of Cultural Studies,
  79–80, 81

Bourdieu, Pierre, 64
Butler, Judith, 55

Cambridge Historians, 52
canonical texts, 73, 91, 93–94, 113–14,
  117, 127. *See also* monuments
capitalism, 78–79
Casey, Caroline, 78, 81–82
causality, 36, 51, 61, 72
censorship, 120
Chouliaraki, Lilie, 36
"The Clash of Civilizations," 91
class, 81
close reading, 103
Cohn, Carol, 18, 52, 114–16
colluded self, 78–79
colonialism, 88, 106–7, 112
Comaroff, Jean, 106
Comaroff, John, 106
common sense, 47, 52
conflict, 92–93
Congo: identity and, 8, 87–88, 95–96, 99,
  104–5, 107; materiality and, 74; representations of, 4, 84, 94, 98–99, 100,
  117, 119
Connolly, William, 48
Conrad, Joseph, 91, 133n1
consciousness, 29
constitutive outside, 89
contextualization, 106
Critical Discourse Analysis, 34–38, 39,
  41, 61
critical realists, 35
critical theory, 27

cultural artifacts, 120
cultural competence, 83–85, 127
cultural myths, 132n2
cultural nation, 123
culture, 63, 64, 66, 79–80, 85, 117, 121

de Beauvoir, Simone, 50–51, 132n1
de Certeau, Michel, 63–64
de Saussure, Ferdinand, 24–25, 55, 71
deconstructive method, 66–67, 109–10
denaturalization, 110
Der Derian, James, 52–54
Derrida, Jacques, 3, 40, 44, 113
description, 36
dialects, 68
diplomacy, 53–54
dirty origin, 53
Discourse, 31
discourse: action and, 60–61, 63, 66; au-
    tochthonous, 76; basic, 105; causality
    and, 36; characteristics of, 51; D. Saco
    and, 18; definition of, 2, 17–21, 62, 125;
    dominance of, 106; Ernesto Laclau
    and, 18; as a framework, 36; gendered,
    114; institutionalization of, 5; interpre-
    tations of, 105–6, 109, 129–130; James
    Paul Gee and, 18, 31–32; Jennifer Mil-
    liken and, 18; Jens Bartleson and, 18;
    knowledge and, 9; language and, 40;
    Laura Shepherd and, 18; mapping of,
    118–21, 128; materiality and, 69;
    meaning-production and, 17, 21;
    methodology of, 14; Michel Foucault
    and, 2, 18, 107; nationalist, 120; nature
    of, 3–4; Norman Fairclough and, 18;
    political, 57; poststructuralism and, 26;
    power and, 58, 128; practice and, 63,
    64, 66; as productive, 51, 52; Roxanne
    Doty and, 18; ruptures in, 105, 127;
    technostrategic, 116; theory of, 14
discourse analysis: benefits of, 11–14; def-
    inition of, 4–9; elastic approach to,
    104–5; genealogical approach to, 21,
    23, 51–53, 67, 69–70, 73, 105, 128,
    131n1; growth of, 1; importance of, 8;
    limitations of, 12; methodologies of,
    19–20, 23–24, 32, 51, 69, 104–5, 126–

28; methodology of, 8, 15; plastic ap-
    proach to, 104; self-reflexivity and,
    129–30; strategies of, 15; visual imag-
    ery and, 131n1
Discourse and Practice (van Leeuwen),
    37
Discourse communities, 31–32
discourse-theoretical analysis, 40
discursive, 35, 36, 61, 103, 105, 108
discursive practices, 45
discursive structures, 40
discursive totalities, 39
domination, 59–60
Doty, Roxanne, 12, 18, 47, 87, 89–90,
    110–11, 126
double reading, 109–10
doxology, 29
Dreyfus, Hubert, 21
du Gay, Paul, 79
Duncan, James, 54
Durkheim, Émile, 26

empirical rigor, 35, 36
empirical study, 52
empiricism, 44, 101
epistemology, 19, 32–33, 34, 36–37, 48,
    61
essentialism, 38
ethics, 54, 72
expectations, 59–60
explanation, 36
extended metaphors, 114
external reality, 35
extradiscursive, 35, 36, 38

Fairclough, Norman, 18, 36, 81–82
Faking It (Weber), 47–48
feminism, 71–72, 77, 92, 115–16
foreign policy, 8, 107–9, 117
Foucault, Michel: action and, 68; class
    and, 81; criminality and, 78; Critical
    Discourse Analysis and, 39; discourse
    and, 2, 18, 20–21, 107; discursive prac-
    tices and, 45; Edward Said and, 50, 74;
    foreign policy and, 107; Frankfurt
    School and, 27–28; government and,
    65, 132n5; governmentality and, 65;

knowledge and, 71–72; linguistic studies and, 9; methodology of, 21–23, 69–70, 123, 131n1; operationalization and, 51; postpositivism and, 28–29; poststructuralism and, 39, 125–26; power and, 48, 54, 56, 65, 132n5; representation and, 27; source selection and, 101; texts and, 91; Theo van Leeuwen and, 37; truth and, 40, 71
Frankfurt School, 24, 27–28
Fukuyama, Francis, 93

Gee, James Paul, 18, 30–32
Geertz, Clifford, 106
gender, 121
gendered, 111, 114
genealogical method, 21, 23, 51–53, 67, 69–70, 73, 105, 131n1
Genealogy of Morals (Nietzsche), 53
A Genealogy of Sovereignty (Bartelson), 70–73
genocide, 109
genre, 96
government, 97, 132n5
governmentality, 65, 66
grammar, 30
Gramsci, Antonio, 117

Habermas, Jürgen, 28
habitus, 64
Hall, Stuart, 50
Hansen, Lene, 67–68, 97, 105–6, 107–9, 112, 114
Heart of Darkness (Conrad), 91, 94, 98, 119, 133n1
hegemony, 58, 117
history of thought, 29
home blind, 85, 94
Humphreys, P., 37
Huntington, Samuel, 91
Huysmans, Jef, 97

identity, 49, 68, 89, 90, 98, 105, 107, 108, 113–14, 123
Imagining the Congo (Dunn), 100–101, 104
imperial encounters, 89–90

Imperial Encounters (Doty), 47–48, 87, 89–90
institutionalization, 5, 46, 59
institutions, 69, 77–78, 91, 97, 125
internalization, 110
International Relations (IR) school, 47
interpellation, 50–51
interpretation, 36
intersubjectivity, 25
intertextual models, 108
intertextuality, 25, 46, 104, 109
An Introduction to Discourse Analysis: Theory and Method (Gee), 30–31

Jackson, Richard, 98
joyful positivism, 29
juvenile delinquency, 5–7, 10–11, 13, 44–46, 91, 122, 126–28, 133n1
juxtapositional method, 67

knowledge: authoritative, 58; background, 110–11; discourse and, 2, 9; discourses and, 61; Michel de Certeau and, 63; Michel Foucault and, 71–72; power and, 3, 48; production of, 66, 126; representations and, 55; social reality, 9; specialized, 95; subjugated, 4, 51
knowledge production, 47, 51
Kress, Gunther, 34
Kuhn, Thomas, 33
Kulturnation, 123

Laclau, Ernesto, 18, 39–40, 62, 90, 113, 122
laddism, 80–81
Lacanian psychoanalysis, 47–48
language: action and, 44–45; definition of, 2; dialects of, 68; discourse analysis and, 6; Ferdinand de Saussure and, 71; institutions and, 69; James Paul Gee and, 31; linguistics and, 30; materiality and, 67–68; meaning and, 24, 44–45; Michel Foucault and, 28–39; positivism and, 44; poststructuralism and, 43–44, 54; practice and, 61; reality and, 35, 40; as relational, 55; social and, 61–62; structure of, 131n2; truth and, 2

language-in-use. *See* discourse
latent structure, 22, 26, 79, 125–26
Latour, Bruno, 76, 77
Learning to Labour (Willis), 79–81
Lévi-Strauss, Claude, 22, 26, 125
Lincoln, Bruce, 132n2
linguistic anthropology, 132n4
linguistic studies, 9, 30–32
linguistic turn, 24, 35, 46, 62, 67
linguistics, 25
literary theory, 74
Lobo-Guerrero, Luis, 87
long conversations, 106
ludic, 92
Lukes, Steven, 55–56
Lumumba, Patrice, 95, 107, 112
Lyotard, Jean-François, 28

manifest structures, 22, 26, 125–26
marginalization, 5, 105
Marx, Karl, 75
Marxism, 56, 79
master signifiers, 113, 116–17
material production, 79
materialist determinism, 81
materiality: Caroline Casey and, 82; dis-
    course and, 67–75; meaning and, 62,
    103, 122; practice and, 3–4; reception
    of, 75
Mauss, Marcel, 26
Mbembe, Achille, 58–60
meaning: consensual, 37; cultural compe-
    tence and, 84; definition of, 44–45; ma-
    teriality and, 2, 62, 103; social world
    and, 17; structure of, 106; transference
    of, 114
meaning-production, 2, 4, 6, 21, 43, 125
means of production, 78
memory, 120
metaphorical analysis, 114–15
metaphors, 104, 114–15, 127
metis, 63–64
Milliken, Jennifer: cultural myths and,
    132n2; discourse and, 18, 54; genealog-
    ical method and, 67; methodology of,
    91; operationalization and, 51; predica-
    tion and, 111; source selection and,
    101; texts and, 112–13

Mills, Sue, 77
monument critique, 50
monuments, 93–94, 113–14, 117, 127
morality, 91
Mouffe, Chantal, 39–40, 62, 90, 113, 122
Mutlu, Can E., 104, 130
myths, 132n2

narcissism, 78–79
National Geographic, 100–101
nationalism, 120
natural facts, 6, 111
naturalization, 2, 65, 85, 90, 110
Newbury, David, 98
Nietzsche, Friedrich, 10–11, 20, 53
nodal points, 66, 93–94, 110, 113, 116–17
nondiscursive. *See* extradiscursive

objectification, 74, 82
observable reality, 29–30
Occident, 74
odnako, 84
On Diplomacy (Der Derian), 52–54
ontology, 19, 32–33, 34, 36–37, 39, 41, 72
operationalization, 51
The Order of Things (Foucault), 21–23,
    26
Orientalism, 91
Orientalism (Said), 12, 47–50, 73–74
orientalists, 74
orientations, 59–60
Other, 4, 48, 49, 72, 89, 92, 112, 114
Othering, 107

participant observation, 116
perception, 33, 45–46, 46, 56
perspective, 115
phenomenology, 33, 46, 53
philosophy of knowledge, 101
policies, 60, 105, 123
political cartoons, 101
politics, 70, 71, 97
The Politics of Insecurity (Huysmans), 97
positivism, 28, 29–30, 34, 34–35, 44, 45–
    46
postcolonial dramaturgy, 59
postcolonial studies, 50, 59, 77
post-Marxism, 79

postpositivism, 10–11, 24, 28–30, 34, 40–41

poststructuralism: causality and, 51, 61; Critical Discourse Analysis and, 35, 35–36, 38; description of, 41; discourse and, 9, 14, 17; discourse analysis and, 39–41; Frankfurt School and, 27–28; identity and, 89; James Paul Gee and, 27–28; language and, 43–44, 54; Michel Foucault and, 9; Other and, 89; power and, 55; Self and, 89; self-reflexivity and, 129; structuralism and, 22, 26–27, 117, 125–26; truth and, 129

power: culture and, 117; discourse and, 54–58, 58, 66; government and, 65; knowledge and, 3, 48; Michel Foucault and, 132n5; representation and, 93

Power: A Radical View (Lukes), 55

power/knowledge nexus, 48

practice, 59; Bourdieu and, 64; characteristics of, 65; common, 37; creation of, 64–65; discourse and, *63*, 64, *66*, 125; as discursive, 61; as integrative, 65; materiality and, 3–4; Michel Foucault and, 2; as quotidian, 65–66; social, 39; structure and, 64, 65

practice theory, 62

predication, 111–12

presupposition, 110–11

primary sources, 99

Pring, Richard, 35

"Provisional Notes on the Postcolony" (Mbembe), 58–60

psychoanalysis, 47–48

publishing, 68

pudenda origo, 53

qualitative, 9–10

quantitative, 9–10

Queer Theory, 47–48

queercore, 84, 132n6

Rabinow, Paul, 21

race, 60, 120, 128

realists, 35

reality, 2, 40, 91, 125

reconceptualization, 62

recontextualization, 37–38

reflexive adaptation, 79

religion, 71

representations: asymmetries of, 103; changes of, 121–23; Congolese, 100–101; context for, 118; contextualization of, 106; Critical Discourse Analysis of, 37–38; cultural competence and, 84; definition of, 33–34; differences in, 7–8, 119; discourse and, 47, 58; Edward Said and, 73; ideal-types of, 105; importance of, 110–11; interpellation and, 50–51; inventorying of, 103–4, 116–18; Othering and, 49; permanence of, 121–24; popular, 97; power and, 58; practice and, 60–67; reality and, 93; research topics and, 8; Roland Barthes and, 46; Russian, 85–86, 110–11; stability of, 118; truth and, 55

research topics: authorial decisions and, 95; journals and, 96; limitations of, 87; reader perspective and, 94–95, 127; refinement of, 88, 94–95, 100–101; selection of, 83, 86–87, 126, 128; source selection for, 7–8, 90–94, 96–97, 99, 100–101, 126; use of texts for, 91

resistance, 57, 60, 88, 89–90

"Rumble in the Jungle," 88

Russia: discourse and, 120; foreign policy of, 8, 83–86; identity and, 92, 110–12, 123; representations and, 96, 104

Said, Edward: colonialism and, 57–58; discourse and, 77; importance of, 12; International Relations (IR) school and, 47–50; Othering and, 73–74; Roxanne Doty and, 89; secondary sources and, 99; texts and, 91

Salter, Mark B., 104, 130

Schatzki, Theodore, 62

schema, 104, 127

scientific rigor, 35

scientific truth, 40–41

Scott, James C., 63, 80

secondary sources, 99

Security as Practice: Discourse Analysis and the Bosnian War (Hansen), 107–9

Self, 4, 76, 89, 92, 112

self-reflexivity, 49, 78, 129–130
semiotic perspective, 115
senses, 32–33
"Sex and Death in the Rational World of
    Defense Intellectuals" (Cohn), 52, 115–
    16
Shapiro, Michael, 34, 44–45
Shepherd, Laura, 18, 66, 113
signifiers, 113
signifying chain, 3
Silverstein, Michael, 132n4
Simulating Sovereignty (Weber), 47–48
Skinner, Quentin, 52
slaves, 119
Slavophiles, 94
social, 36, 61–62
social facts, 26–27
social linguistics, 30–31
social reality, 33, 48
Somer, Margaret, 65
sovereignty, 47, 70, 71, 72, 76, 88, 105
sports, 18–19
Stanley, Henry Morten, 93–94
state power, 59–60
Stowe, Harriet Beecher, 91
straightedge, 132n6
structuralism: Claude Lévi-Strauss and,
    22, 79; Critical Discourse Analysis and,
    34–35, 39; critique of, 26; description
    of, 24–27; Karl Marx and, 79; post-
    structuralism and, 14, 17, 22, 117,
    125
structures, 29, 40, 64, 65
subaltern, 77
subject positions, 75–76, 77–78, 112–14
subjugated method, 67
superstructure, 79–80
surface, 29
Swidler, Ann, 62–63
sXe, 84, 132n6
Sylvan, David, 111

taboos, 78
Tarzan, 98
Tatars, 5, 92, 110–11

technologies of government, 97
technostrategic discourses, 116
temporal perspective, 108
tendencies, 38
testability, 35
texts: canonical, 73, 91, 113–14, 117, 127;
    close reading of, 103; competing narra-
    tives, 99–100; definition of, 44, 46;
    ideal-types, 105–6; ignored, 96–97; im-
    portance of, 101; interrelatedness of,
    92, 108; manuals and, 73; materiality
    and, 69; official, 97; political, 97
textual, 36
thick description, 106
Tintin in the Congo, 98
Todorov, Tzvetan, 113
Torfing, Jacob, 23, 40
transcendental centre, 40
transhistorical, 53
trans-linguistics, 25
transparency, 130
tropes, 104, 119, 127
truth, 2, 47, 57, 71, 73, 129–30
truth-effect, 113

Uncle Tom's Cabin, 91
Uses of the Other, 104
utilitarian, 92
utterances, 20, 22, 63, 79, 90

Van Dijk, T., 41
van Leeuwen, Theo, 34, 37, 37–38
Verfassungspatriotismus, 123
visual imagery, 131n1

Weber, Cynthia, 47–48
Weldes, Jutta, 18, 50
Westernizers, 94
White, Hayden, 114
Will to Power (Nietzsche), 10–11
Willis, Paul, 79–81
Wittgenstein, Ludwig, 31
worldviews, 33
Writing the War on Terrorism (Jackson),
    98

Made in the USA
Middletown, DE
14 January 2020

83206458R00094